THE EROTIC SENTIMENT
In the Paintings of China and Japan

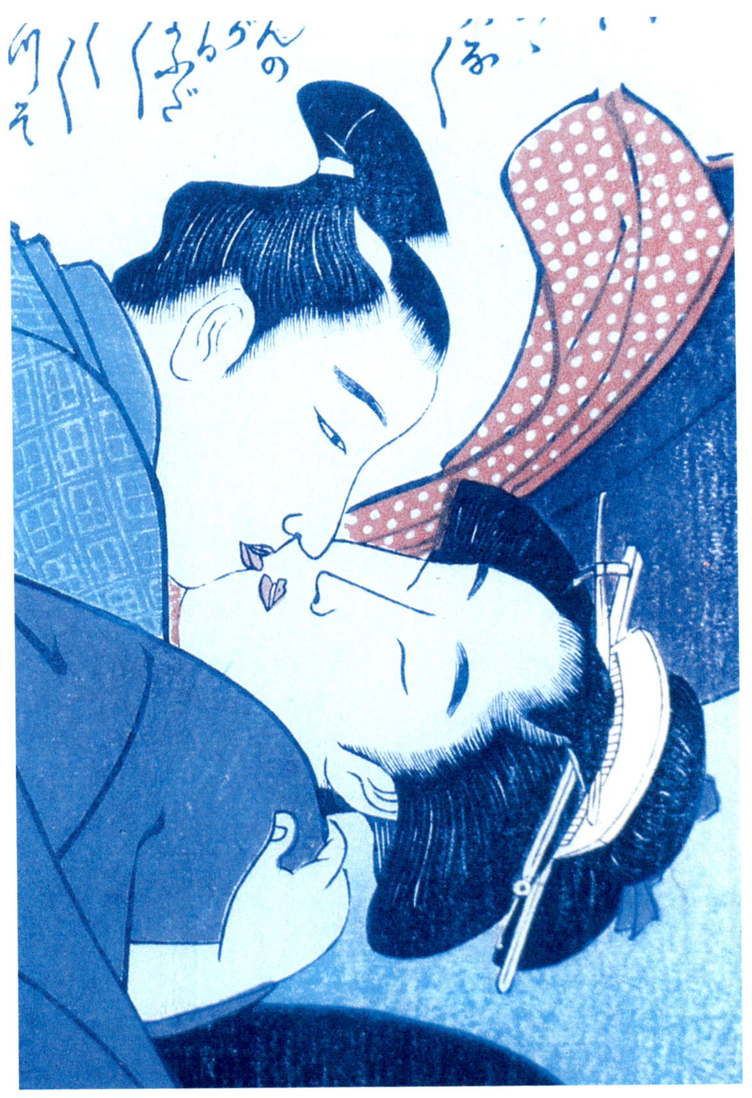

Of all things that make people prosper, none can be compared to the act of love.

I-shin-po

The Erotic Sentiment

In the
Paintings of China and Japan

Nik Douglas and

Penny Slinger

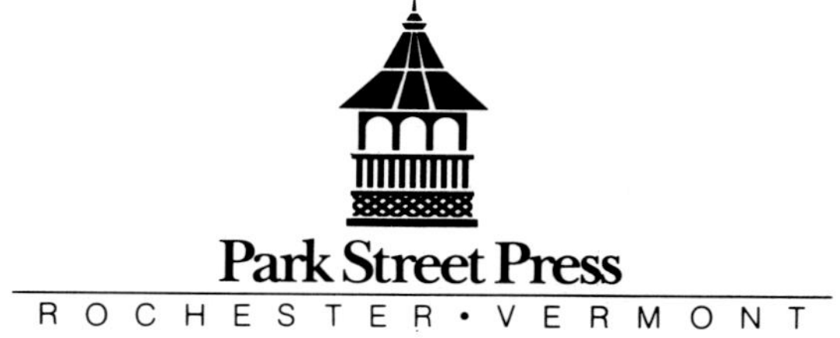

Park Street Press
ROCHESTER · VERMONT

Park Street Press
One Park Street
Rochester, Vermont 05767

Library of Congress Cataloging-in-Publication Data

Douglas, Nik.
The erotic sentiment in the paintings of China & Japan.
Rev. ed. of: The pillow book. c1981
Includes bibliographical references.
1. Erotic painting, Chinese. 2. Erotic painting, Japanese
I. Slinger, Penny, 1947–   II. Douglas, Nik.
Pillow book.   III. Title.
ND 1460.E75D68   1988   757'.8'095   88-30887
ISBN 0-89281-495-0

Printed and bound in Hong Kong

10 9 8 7 6 5 4 3 2 1

Park Street Press is a division of Inner Traditions International

Distributed to the book trade in Canada by Publishers Group West (PGW), Toronto, Ontario
Distributed to the book trade in the United Kingdom by Deep Books, London
Distributed to the book trade in Australia by Millennium Books, Newtown, N. S. W.
Distributed to the book trade in New Zealand by Tandem Press, Auckland

CONTENTS

LIST OF COLOR PLATES

15 Album painting on silk, China, late 18th/early 19th century, size: 20 × 24.5 cm. **16** Album painting on silk, China, late 18th century, size: 35 × 39 cm. **17** Album painting on silk, China, late 19th century, size: 16.2 × 19.8 cm. **18** Album painting on silk, China, late 18th century, size: 34.5 × 38.5 cm. **19** Album painting on silk, China, late 18th century, size: 34.8 × 38.9 cm. **20** Album painting on silk, China, late 18th/early 19th century, size: 20 × 24.5 cm. **21** Album painting on silk, China, late 18th century, size: 28.8 × 32.5 cm. **22** Watercolor on rice paper, China, late 19th century, size: 15.3 × 20.4 cm. **23** Album painting on silk, China, 19th century, size: 20.2 × 26.2 cm. **24** Scroll painting on silk, China, late 18th/early 19th century, size: 20.1 × 20.9 cm. **25** Shunga painting on silk, Meiji, Japan, 19th century, size: 18.7 × 22.1 cm. **26** Album painting on silk, China, 19th century, size: 16.2 × 20 cm. **27** Shunga print, Meiji, Japan, School of Utamaro, early 19th century, size: 25.1 × 35.1 cm. **28** Watercolor on paper, China, late 19th century, size: 18.9 × 21.4 cm. **29** Shunga painting on silk, Meiji, Japan, 19th century, size: 18.7 × 22 cm. **30** Album painting on silk, China, late 19th century, size: 16.3 × 20.1 cm. **31** Shunga print, Meiji, Japan, School of Utamaro, early 19th century, size: 25 × 35 cm. **32** Album painting on silk, China, 19th century, size: 20.2 × 26.2 cm. **33** Shunga print, Japan, 18th century, size: 22 × 31.2 cm. **34** Album painting on silk, China, late 19th century, size: 16.3 × 20 cm. **35** Album painting on silk, China, 19th century, size: 20.2 × 26.2 cm. **36** Shunga painting on silk, Meiji, Japan, 19th century, size: 18.8 × 22 cm. **37** Shunga print, Meiji, Japan, School of Utamaro, early 19th century, size: 25 × 35.2 cm. **38** Scroll painting on silk, China, late 18th/early 19th century, size: 20.1 × 20.9 cm. **39** Shunga painting on silk, Meiji, Japan, 19th century, size: 18.7 × 22.1 cm. **40** Album painting on silk, China, late 18th century, size: 34.7 × 39 cm. **41** Shunga print, Japan, 18th century, size: 22 × 33 cm. **42** Album painting on silk, China, late 19th century, size: 16.3 × 20 cm. **43** Album painting on silk, China, late 19th century, size: 16.2 × 20 cm. **44** Album painting on silk, China, 19th century, size: 20.2 × 26.2 cm. **45** Album painting on silk, China, 19th century, size: 20.2 × 26.2 cm. **46** Watercolor on paper, China, late 19th century, size: 18.9 × 21.4 cm. **47** Scroll painting on silk, China, late 18th/early 19th century, size: 20.1 × 20.9 cm. **48** Album painting on silk, China, late 19th century, size: 16.2 × 20 cm. **48** Album painting on silk, China, late 19th century, size: 16.2 × 19.9 cm. **49** Watercolor on paper, China, late 19th century, size: 18.9 × 21.4 cm. **50** Album painting on silk, China, late 18th century, size: 28.6 × 32.5 cm. **51** Album painting on silk, China, 19th century, size: 30.1 × 30.1 cm. **52** Album painting on silk, China, late 19th century, size: 16.4 × 20.1 cm. **53** Album painting on silk, China, 19th century, size: 20.2 × 26.2 cm. **54** Watercolor on paper, China, late 19th century, size: 18.9 × 21.4 cm. **55** Album painting on silk, China, late 18th/early 19th century, size: 20 × 24.5 cm. **56** Watercolor on rice paper, China, late 19th century, size: 16.3 × 20.8 cm. **57** Scroll paintings on silk, China, late 18th/early 19th century, size each: 20.1 × 20.9 cm. **58** Album painting on silk, China, late 19th century, size: 16.3 × 20.1 cm. **59** Watercolor on rice paper, China, late 19th century, size: 18.9 × 21.4 cm. **60** Watercolor on rice paper, China, late 19th century, size: 18.9 × 21.4 cm. **61** Shunga painting on rice paper, Meiji, Japan, late 18th/early 19th century, size: 27 × 39 cm. **62** Watercolor on rice paper, China, late 19th century, size: 16.3 × 20.7 cm. **63** Shunga painting on rice paper, Japan, late 18th century, size: 23.4 × 37.5 cm. **64** Album painting on silk, China, 19th century, size: 18.5 × 22.5 cm. **65** Scroll painting on silk, China, late 18th/early 19th century, size: 20.1 × 20.9 cm. **66** Album painting on silk, China, 19th century, size: 30.1 × 30 cm. **67** Scroll painting on silk, China, late 18th/early 19th century, size: 20.1 × 20.9 cm. **68** Album painting on silk, China, late 19th century, size: 14.7 × 16.7 cm. **69** Album painting on silk, China, 19th century, size: 30.2 × 30 cm. **70** Album painting on silk, China, late 19th century, size: 16.8 × 19.8 cm. **71** Album painting on silk, China, late 19th century, size: 16.3 × 20 cm. **72** Album painting on silk, China, late 19th century, size: 16.4 × 20.1 cm. **73** Album painting on silk, China, late 19th century, size: 16.4 × 20.1 cm. **74** Album painting on silk, China, late 19th/early 20th century, size: 12.6 × 15.7 cm. **75** Album painting on silk, China, late 19th/early 20th century, size: 12.8 × 15.8 cm. **76** Album painting on silk, China, late 18th/early 19th century, size: 19.8 × 24.3 cm. **77** Album painting on silk, China, late 18th century, 34.6 × 39 cm. **78** Album painting on silk, China, late 18th/early 19th century, size: 20 × 24.5 cm. **79** Album painting on silk, China, late 19th century, size: 16.2 × 20 cm.

THE EROTIC SENTIMENT
In Chinese and Japanese Culture and Art

*The Bedroom Arts comprise the entire Supreme Way
And can themselves suffice to help one achieve Immortality.
These arts are said to enable a person to avert calamities
And become freed from misdeeds,
Even to change bad luck into good fortune.*

Ko Hung

Since prehistoric times the erotic sentiment has played a major role in the development of Chinese and Japanese culture and influenced its art. According to ancient Chinese cosmology, it was the mating of Heaven and Earth, as a great storm, which created the first humans. Japanese creation myths, too, tell how Izanagi, "the male who invites," and Isanami, "the female who invites," came to Earth, learned the art of love by watching a pair of wagtail birds mating, and so inspired, created the Japanese islands. Phallic shrines were an essential ingredient of early Shinto religion, and depictions of Japanese household deities in sexual union were believed to bring good luck and health. Even in present-day Japan, enormous phalluses are paraded through the towns during certain festivals, and depictions of the sexual organs are generally considered auspicious.

The father of Chinese civilization, the "Yellow Emperor" Huang-Ti (third millenium B.C.), is credited with treatises on medicine and sex, inscribed on bamboo and tortoise shells. As the "Son of Heaven," the Emperor was held responsible for everything that went on in his kingdom, including control of the weather, rain-making, the fertility of crops, and the general health of his people. The Emperor's sexual activities were believed to influence directly the health and longevity of both himself and his kingdom. Thus,

it was very important that he be a master of the arts of love. An important Taoist text states:

The Emperor rules over all the complications
   of the Empire,
Therefore he must familiarize himself with the
   disciplines of Tao.
Part of his duty lies in the harem,
So he must know the correct methods of sexual
   action.
The principle of this method is to have frequent
   acts of sex
But emit his essence only on rare occasions.
This method makes a man's body light and will
   expel all diseases.

Su-nu-ching

Essentially matriarchal in its philosophy of life, Taoism evolved through close observation of Nature. The Tao, "The Way," recognized the order of Nature throughout the universe—in causality, change, and the interplay of the female and male cosmic principles of Yin and Yang. Thus, it is to Nature that one must look for the inspirations and symbols for the erotic sentiment in Chinese culture.

The Supreme Tao was compared to water: flowing, yielding, "submissive,"and linked to the vital principle of femininity. In ancient China many of the shamans (Ch: Wu) were women, and dancing and rain-making were some of their principal functions. Legend tells how a prince, intending to visit the Mountain of Shamans, fell asleep on the way there. In his dream he met a woman of extraordinary grace and beauty, who declared herself to be the Lady of the Mountain and proceeded to initiate him into the mysteries of sex. As she left the prince, the lady said, "I am she who brings the clouds in the morning; I am she who evokes the rain in the evening." The popular Chinese expression for love-making, Clouds and Rain (Ch: Yun-yu), is linked to this legend.

During the great Yin, or Shang, Dynasty, which lasted until about 1100 B.C., Taoists developed many techniques for harmonizing with Nature, including dietary, respiratory, gymnastic, heliotherapeutic, pharmaceutical, and sexual methods. Collectively, these methods were referred to as "nourishing Nature." The sexual act was viewed as part of Nature's order, and proper sexual practices were considered the sacred duty of every man and woman, without which it was believed that calamaties would result.

The union of man and woman is like the mating
    of Heaven and Earth.
It is because of their correct mating that Heaven
    and Earth last forever.
Humans have lost this secret and have therefore
    become mortal.
By knowing it the Path to Immortality is opened.
Shang-ku-san-tai

The *I-ching*, or "Book of Changes" (probably compiled towards the end of the Yin Dynasty), describes Yin and Yang as dual cosmic forces that perpetuate the universe. An ancient commentary on the *I-ching* declares:

The constant intermingling of Heaven and Earth
Gives shape to all things.
The sexual union of man and woman
Gives life to all things.

In Chinese culture, pure eroticism was always linked to the deep philosophical and romantic notions of Taoism. Writers, poets, and artists all looked to Nature for erotic inspiration and analogy. The fertilizing of Earth by Heaven, the longing of the dry Earth for rain, the bursting of clouds and the pouring of rain, ripe delicate fruits, full blossoms, high mountains, deep valleys, rushing waterfalls, still pools, the Spring season, the mating of animals and birds—all were symbols of the erotic sentiment to the Chinese and when brought together as erotic ingredients in a work of art or literature were very effective in establishing an atmosphere charged with sexual promise and meaning.

Classical Chinese erotic writings have the charming custom of using poetic names to refer to the sexual organs, the act of sex, sexual postures, and the sexual fluids. Such erotic nomenclature included, for the male organ, the Jade Branch, Dragon Pillar, Yang Pagoda, Crimson Bird, Ambassador, Most Precious Thing; for the female organ, the Jade Gate, Pleasure Grotto, Shady Valley, Grotto of the White Tiger, Cinnabar Crevice, Anemone, Golden Furrow, Honey Pot, Peach, Precious Shell. The act of sex was referred to as Clouds and Rain, Visiting the Wu Mountain, the Battle of Love, or the Secret Rite. Among names for the sexual postures we find Turning Dragon, Fluttering Phoenix, Cranes with Joined Necks, Jumping Wild Horses, Gobbling Fishes, Fluttering Butterfly Searching for Flowers, Queen Bee Making Honey, Floating Porpoises, Over the Rainbow, Floating Turtle, and Standing Bamboos. The male juice of love was termed the Yang Fluid, Jade Juice, or Pearl Essence; the female secretions, the Yin Fluid, Moon Flower Waters, Peach Juice, Melon Juice, or Fountain Waters. Menstruation was the Monthly Affair or Monthly Guest, and menstrual fluid the Regular Fluid, Peach Flower Flow, Red Flood, or Red Snow. Male homosexuality was referred to as Reverse Clouds and Inverted Rain, and female homosexuality was termed Doubling Nature or Nourishing Yin.

By about the fifth century B.C. the sage Lao Tzu brought together the essential precepts of Taoism in a small book known as the *Tao Te Ching*. Taoists condemned class and sex discrimination, promoted mysticism and magic, and emphasized the natural healing power of the elements and the feminine principle. A text of the fifth century B.C. declares:

8

Water is yielding, submissive, and clean,
and likes to wash away the evils of man.
This may be called its "benevolence."
Human beings are made mostly of water.
The seminal essence of man and the life-juice
    of the woman unite,
and water flows, forming a new shape.
The sage's transformation arises from solving
    the problems and mysteries of water.
If water is known and united, the human heart
    will be corrected.

Kuan Tzu

During the Chou Dynasty (circa 800–200 B.C.), the philosophy of Confucius (Ch: Khung Fu Tzu) was established, promoting democratic and patriarchal ideals. By the early Han Dynasty (circa 200 B.C.), though the cult in the palace was mainly Taoist, Confucianism had become the official doctrine of intellectuals and the bureaucracy, a state cult focusing especially on acceptable "custom," status, and ancestor worship; it all but did away with the priesthood (both male and female) and had no time at all for mysticism.

Confucius regarded hermits and Taoist mystics as irresponsible and socially unacceptable, and although he incorporated Taoist viewpoints and terminology in his philosophy, he redefined them and used them differently.

Confucianism was essentially opposed to Taoism and its matriarchal foundation; its influence in both China and Japan has lasted until the present. This philosophy had a profound effect on sexual practices, especially those of a mystical type or those in which the woman took an active or dominant role. The popular idea of the oriental woman as subservient and the "property" of man is directly derived from the Confucian definition of woman's role in the household. Man was viewed as the head of the family, and woman was considered inferior, useful only to work or to bear sons. Confucius' *Li-chi*, or "Book of Rites," declares that a man should not sexually neglect any of his wives or concubines, and the Confucian approach to sex was regulatory in this respect, rather than celebratory, with much emphasis on the need for separation of the sexes in everyday life.

Most of the Han Emperors patronized Confucianism, and affairs of the palace were generally organized by the eunuchs. As the Han Dynasty progressed, the economic situation deteriorated rapidly, drought and famine arose, and eventually the common people revolted, led by Taoist priests. This revolt was finally crushed, and as a result, Chinese patriarchy was even more firmly established.

By the middle of the first century A.D., Buddhism had been introduced into China by Indian monks under the protection of a Han prince, who was also a patron of Taoism. Several Buddhist texts were circulated, and Buddhist art began to flourish. Teachings of several different schools of Buddhism were introduced over the next centuries, including those of the *Hinayana* ("Lesser Vehicle"), which focused on the spiritual salvation of the individual, and the *Mahayana* ("Greater Vehicle"), which emphasized spiritual salvation for all. In the early sixth century, the Indian monk Bodhidharma brought the Ch'an sect to China. Ch'an practices emphasized mysticism and contemplation and greatly influenced Chinese art and culture. By the thirteenth century, this Buddhist sect had reached Japan, and became well established there. Eventually it became better known as Zen Buddhism, the art and poetry of which have received wide attention.

By the eighth century the *Vajrayana* ("Diamond Vehicle") of Indian Buddhist Tantrism was established in China. Soon, many Tantras and other esoteric mystical texts were translated into Chinese, and Tantric paintings, diagrams, and sculpture were produced in China. At the beginning of the ninth century, the Japanese Buddhist monk Kukai pursued esoteric study in China and returned to Japan with Tantric practices and related arts. Buddhist mystic phrases, diagrams, gestures, syllables, multi-armed peaceful and wrathful deities, and mandalas subsequently became incorporated into Japanese art and culture, and it seems likely that Tantric sexual techniques were also introduced during this period.

It is difficult to know how much influence Tantric Buddhist cults have had on expressions of the erotic sentiment in everyday China and Japan.

9

Generally speaking, Tantric Buddhism is closer to Taoism than Confucianism; many of the mystical, contemplative, and sexual practices of some of its cults are almost indistinguishable from those of Taoism. What seems certain is that the introduction of Tantric Buddhism to both China and Japan helped counteract the extremes of Confucianism and may have kept the mystical and spiritual leanings of the people alive. The twelfth-century historical commentator Hu Yin categorically stated that "ice and glowing coals would mix better than Confucianism and Buddhism," and history documents the strained relations between those two philosophies of life.

By the Mongol, or Yuan, Dynasty (A.D. 1279–1367), Tantric Buddhism of Lamaist origin became the state religion of China, and Tantric painting and sculpture flourished. The Mongol Emperors participated in sexual rites for longevity, which blended traditional Taoist "bedroom arts," Tantric sexual yogic techniques, and pagan mysticism.

An important aspect of both Chinese and Japanese erotic art is that it reflects societies whose aristocracy was largely polygamous. Polygamous sexual scenarios are referred to in Chinese as the Secret Dalliance, and it was proficiency in the art of love which enabled the master of the house to satisfy and harmonize the many mistresses. Lady Pan Chao, a Chinese feminist of the first century, spoke of polygamy in her "Woman's Precepts":

Woman has four qualities, namely womanly attainments, womanly speech, womanly appearance, and womanly skills. According to the Rites Man has the right to marry more than one wife, but woman shall not follow two masters. For it is said: "A husband is Heaven, and Heaven cannot be shirked."
Nu-chieh

The view that Heaven cannot or should not be shirked, though very much a part of Chinese tradition, was not always held. The Taoist goddess Hsi-Wang-mu, who presided over the Western Paradise where the "Peach of Immortality" grew, supposedly obtained immortality by practicing Taoist love-secrets. She nurtured her Yin-essence by having many affairs with beautiful young girls, and also made love with innumerable young boys while withholding her own orgasm.

Her secret must not be divulged, lest other women should try to imitate Queen Hsi-Wang-mu's methods. A woman who has learned this secret will feed on her love-making with men and she will prolong her life and not grow old, but always remain like a young girl.
Yu-fang-pi-chuch

Erotic Paintings and Prints from China and Japan

Unfortunately, no early illustrated Chinese sexual handbooks have survived, though references and literary extracts occur from the Han period onwards. During the Sui Dynasty (A.D. 590–618), the existence of many sexual handbooks was recorded, such as "Handbook of Sex of the Dark Girl," "The Secret Art of the Bedchamber," and "Principles of Nurturing Life." These books in the original Chinese have been lost, but long extracts of some of them have survived in Japan in the I-shin-po, a tenth-century compendium of medical science. During the T'ang Dynasty (A.D. 618–907), additional sexual handbooks existed, but apart from a single collector's reference and a brief description of a T'ang Dynasty erotic scroll painting of an Emperor in sexual union with one of his consorts, aided by two ladies and watched by two others, we have little information about this period of erotic art.

A ninth-century sexual handbook known as "Poetical Essay on the Supreme Joy of the Sexual Union of Yin and Yang and Heaven and Earth" includes several references to Buddhism; unfortunately, it is not illustrated, and no illustrated sexual handbooks or erotic scrolls have survived from the Five Dynasties and the Sung period (A.D. 908–1279), although there are many literary and poetic references to erotic themes and scenarios. Prostitutes and courtesans abounded in this period, and those of the higher classes were famous for their skill in all the arts, including dancing, music, poetry, and painting. With the subsequent revival of Confucianism, strict rules were introduced which cramped spontaneity and artistic expression. The Chinese custom of female foot-binding developed at this time.

From very early times, small feet were seen as signs of womanly beauty in Chinese culture. The practice of foot-binding suddenly became fashionable in the twelfth century and lasted until the early twentieth century. The custom is said to have originated with the love poet Li Yu, who made his favorite consort, Yao-niang, compress and bind her feet so that they became pointed like the crescent-ends of the moon; he then had her dance on a large lotus flower which he had constructed. It was said that this event attracted such attention and admiration that other ladies imitated her foot-binding.

Whether or not this event was the real origin of foot-binding, the practice severely restricted a woman's freedom of movement and at the same time altered her gait, making it somewhat resemble the effect of modern-day high heels. Some Chinese writers have suggested that restricted movements became symbolic of womanly modesty and the Confucian ideal, whereas others have declared that the special gait resulting from foot-binding caused a particularly valued development of the female sexual muscles and reflexes. Whatever the truth, from the twelfth century onwards, women were invariably depicted in Chinese art with tiny bound feet, often covered by exquisite leggings. Foot fetishism occurs commonly in Chinese erotic literature from this period onwards. Shoes and leggings were generally kept on during sexual activities, except on special occasions of great intimacy, when feet might be unbound and revealed.

During the Sung Dynasty in China there was a resurgence of interest in Taoism among the aristocracy, and there is mention of "Pictures of Secret Dalliance" and "Spring Pictures," a term that would soon be used to describe Japanese erotic paintings and prints (Jap: Shunga, lit: "Spring drawings"). The earliest surviving examples of Chinese erotic paintings are from the Ming Dynasty (A.D. 1368–1644), when Confu-

cianism once again became the officially recognized philosophy and dominant cultural influence. (Interestingly, it was mostly women who supported Buddhism during this time.)

After the latter part of the sixteenth century, fine erotic paintings on silk or paper were quite common among the Chinese nobility. However, during the Manchu conquest of 1644, most erotic albums were destroyed by government order. During the early eighteenth and nineteenth centuries, erotic paintings re-emerged in "pillow book" format, although they were kept very private and were rarely displayed openly. Pillow books usually presented a series of erotic events in drawings, paintings, or prints. These would then be placed in a particular sequence and mounted on hand scrolls or fold-out albums, or bound into small volumes. Subtle erotic verses or descriptions of erotic activity usually appeared between the illustrations, which would sometimes be embellished with quotations from famous classical treatises on the art of the bedchamber, extracts from famous erotic novels, or esoteric texts pertaining to love.

No really early Japanese Shunga survive except for fragments or sketches, although there are references to them in the literature. The Japanese Abbot Toba (A.D. 1053–1140), a great painter, also painted erotic subjects and utilized the Japanese custom of exaggerating the size of the sexual organs in his art. Greatly enlarged sexual organs are also a feature of very early Japanese art and generally occur as talismans or fertility symbols. That this custom has survived in Shunga paintings and prints indicates the lasting influence of the pagan Shinto religion, with its origin in primitive phallicism.

Japanese erotic illustrations tend to be more dynamic and emotional than the Chinese equivalent, even when identical postures are protrayed. Erotic abandon as well as inventive and humorous sexual scenarios are quite common in Japanese Shunga but are rare in Chinese culture except as illustrations to novels. One of the earliest surviving Japanese erotic scrolls, entitled "The Phallic Contest," humorously shows women sampling and judging greatly exaggerated phalluses. Bound or covered feet are very rarely seen in Japanese erotic art, wherein it is quite common to portray a woman's toes in precise detail as they curl in the ecstasy of fulfillment.

Traditionally, a typical Shunga scroll or book consisted of twelve scenes, said to be linked to the twelve months of the year, although usually the connection was tentative. While the overall effect of Japanese Shunga is somewhat different from that of its Chinese counterpart, which is more reserved and formalized, both were originally inspired by sexological treatises of the early Taoists.

Japanese Shunga had evolved from its archaic form by the late sixteenth century. It recognized a total of forty-eight love postures, taken from the traditional number of different falls in sumo wrestling. Shunga continued to develop along secular lines and drew much of its inspiration from the Ukiyo culture (lit: "this fleeting, floating world"). Like her Indian and Chinese counterparts, the high-class Japanese courtesan was sophisticated, accomplished, and enticing company. She was highly regarded as an asset to society. In her role as a priestess of sex, she exerted tremendous influence, and she inspired many works of art. The famous Ukiyo culture emerged as a culture of eroticism and sensuality within the strict Confucian state culture—a secret society of courtesans, dancers, artists, writers, poets, actors, musicians, scholars, and patrons, all fleeing the constraints of mainstream society.

With the development and perfection of full-color woodblock printing, Shunga could be mass-produced and marketed as entertaining aids to seduction which also had artistic and educational value. Shunga art covers a wide range of sexual scenarios. Most depict heterosexual couples in dalliance or making love, and an occasional group scene with a man and two or more women, but it is not uncommon to find both male and female homosexual activities as well as rape scenes, anal sex (with men and women), and sadomasochism. This feature of Japanese Shunga is unique to oriental erotica as a whole and is probably due to a combination of the strict sexual repression dur-

ing the early Buddhist and Confucian periods and the later popularization of the heroic aggression of the Samurai warriors, many of whom took young men as lovers.

All the original Chinese and Japanese erotic art reproduced in this book was created between the mid-eighteenth and early twentieth centuries. During this time, pictures generally originated as a series combined with erotic poems or quotations; however, such sets were invariably broken up.

Most of our Chinese examples were painted with finely ground mineral pigments mixed with an adhesive medium and applied to a natural-colored silkground, mounted on card, paper, or brocade; the few examples of watercolors were painted on rice paper. Several unusually large and fine paintings on silk, done during the eighteenth century, are published here for the first time. The Japanese examples shown here are paintings on silk and colored woodblock prints on rice paper.

The artists who created these Chinese and Japanese works were truly masters of the erotic sentiment. They combined a delicate palette with spontaneity of line, understanding of space and composition, and attention to detail in such a way that the overall effect is always moving and meaningful. Specific sexual postures, facial expressions, and color combinations, and the inclusion of precise symbolic elements—such as a dragon or phoenix motif, open lotuses, full peonies, bursting blossoms, red candles or columns, stags, and cranes—were carefully blended together according to ancient Taoist tradition.

All the illustrations reproduced here were objects of study during our research for the publication *Sexual Secrets: The Alchemy of Ecstasy* (New York: Destiny Books, 1979). A selection was published in full color in *The Pillow Book: The Erotic Sentiment and the Paintings of India, Nepal, China, and Japan* (New York: Destiny Books, 1981). Although *The Pillow Book* is now out of print, this present volume and its companion, *The Erotic Sentiment: In the Paintings of India and Nepal* (Rochester, Vermont: Park Street Press, 1989), are a response to continued interest in the material.

Nik Douglas

THE EROTIC SENTIMENT
In the Paintings of China and Japan

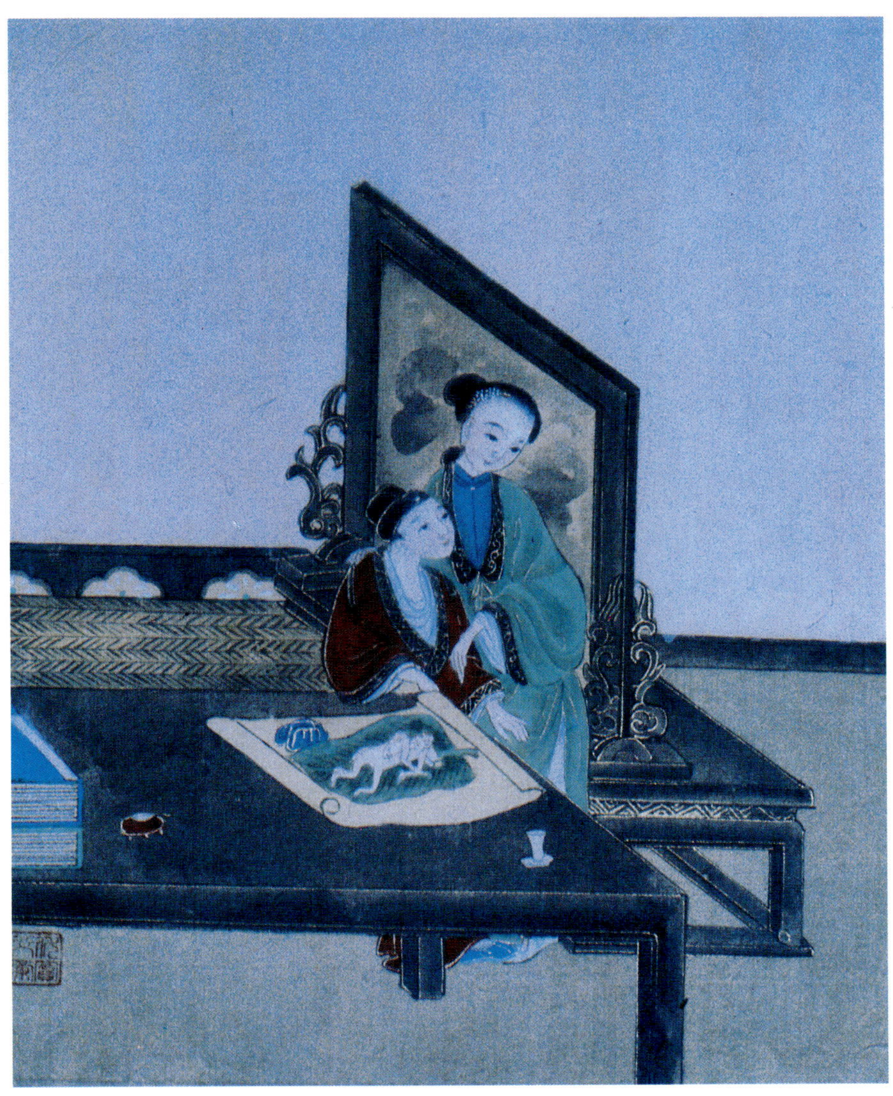

This opening page from a pillow book shows a Chinese noble couple looking at an ancient erotic scroll painting while tenderly caressing each other. Two bound volumes of erotica rest on one side of the table. The palette is of cool mineral colors.

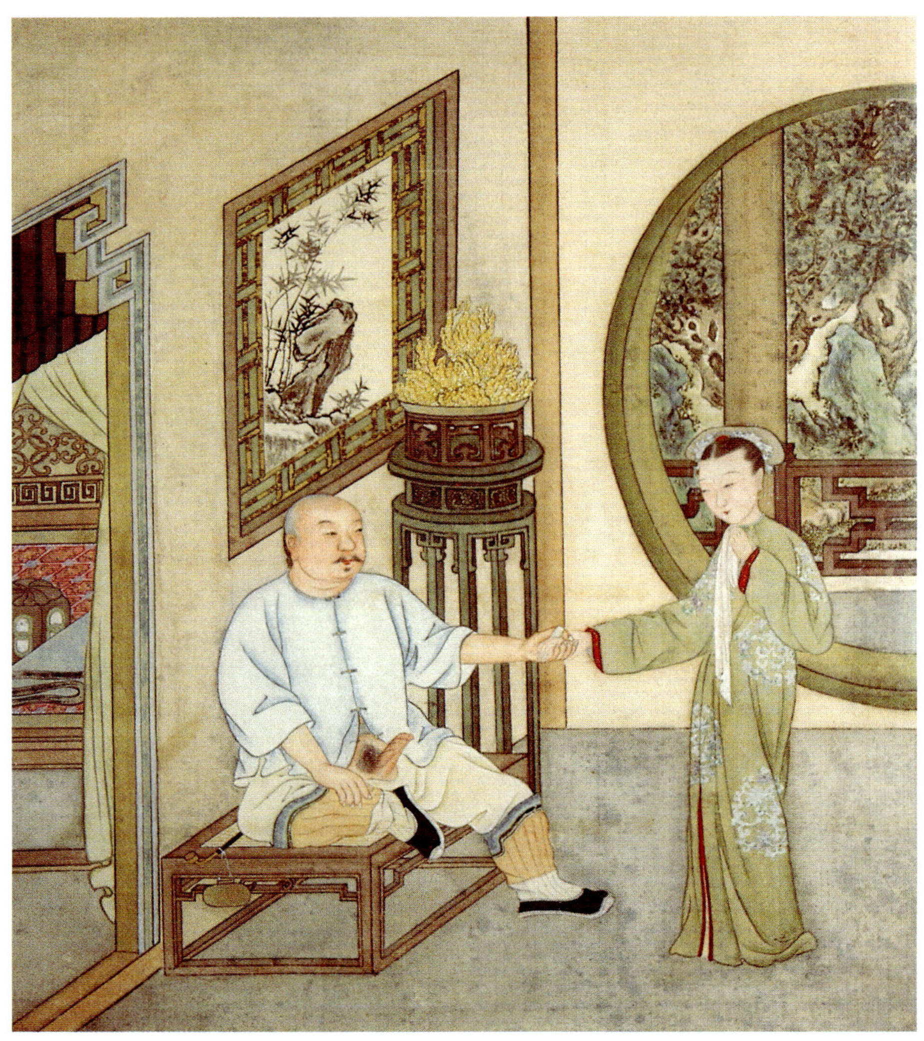

In an unusually large and fine painting, part of a series, a Mandarin is seated on a bench within an ornate stylized Chinese room, an opium pipe at his side and his "Jade Stalk" exposed and erect. He holds a robed noble-lady by the hand. A bed is visible in an adjoining room.

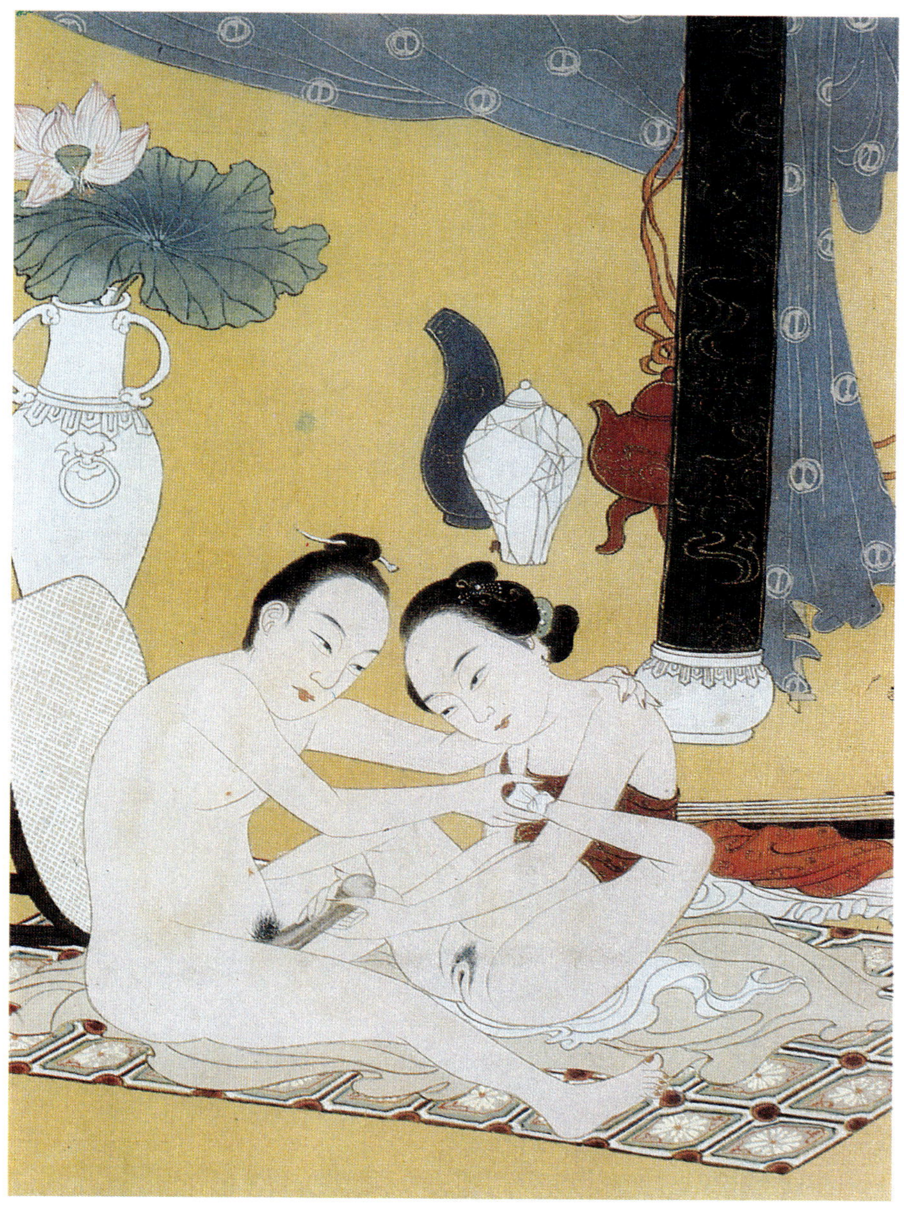

Here an interior scene shows a Chinese couple looking lovingly at each other while engaged in foreplay upon an ornate mat. The woman caresses her partner's "Jade Stalk," while he clasps her tiny foot. Behind them a pink lotus bursts open, suggesting sensual awakening. The subtle hues harmonize with the delicate skin tones, creating a mood of anticipation.

Feasting and sporting with the Living Goddess of Fortune,
Point out the Pictures of Love;
Spending the nights in her precious company,
Observe the sequence of love-images
And enjoy their special qualities.

Poem of the Han dynasty

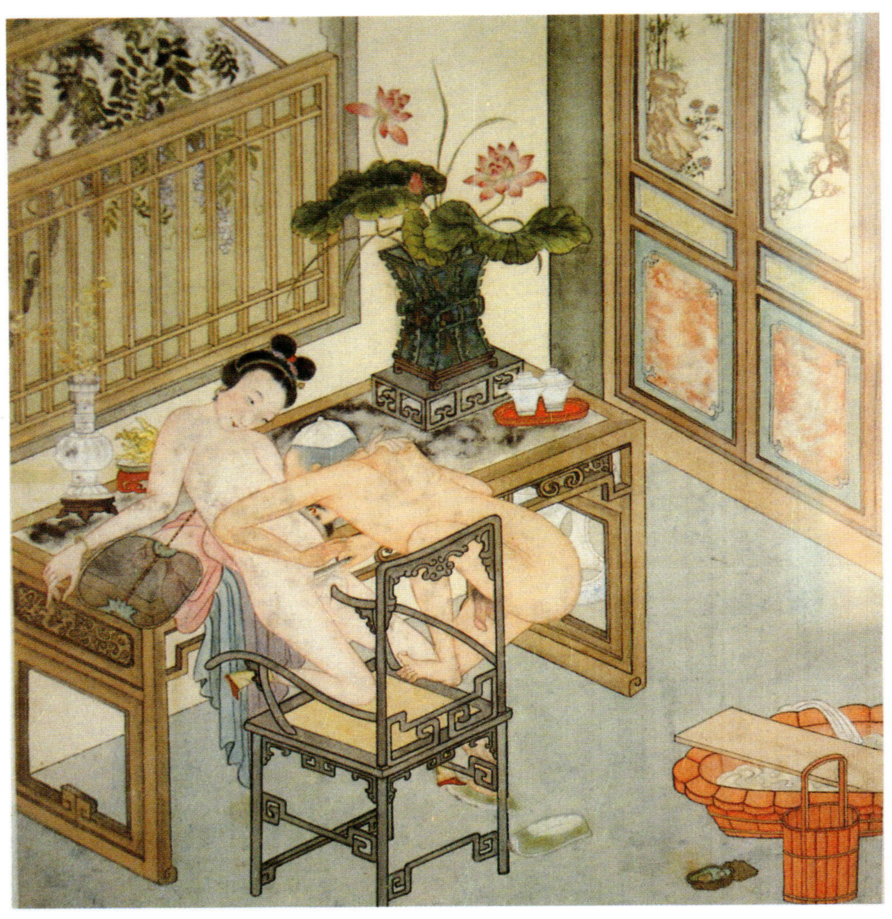

A naked white-skinned Chinese lady kneels on a chair and leans back against a table, a fan by her side, as an elderly naked man wearing a skullcap shaves her pubic hair from her "Grain-Shaped Cave." A washbowl and toilet items are depicted to the right. Lotuses are shown blooming in an ornate vase, and twin teacups rest on a red tray on the table.

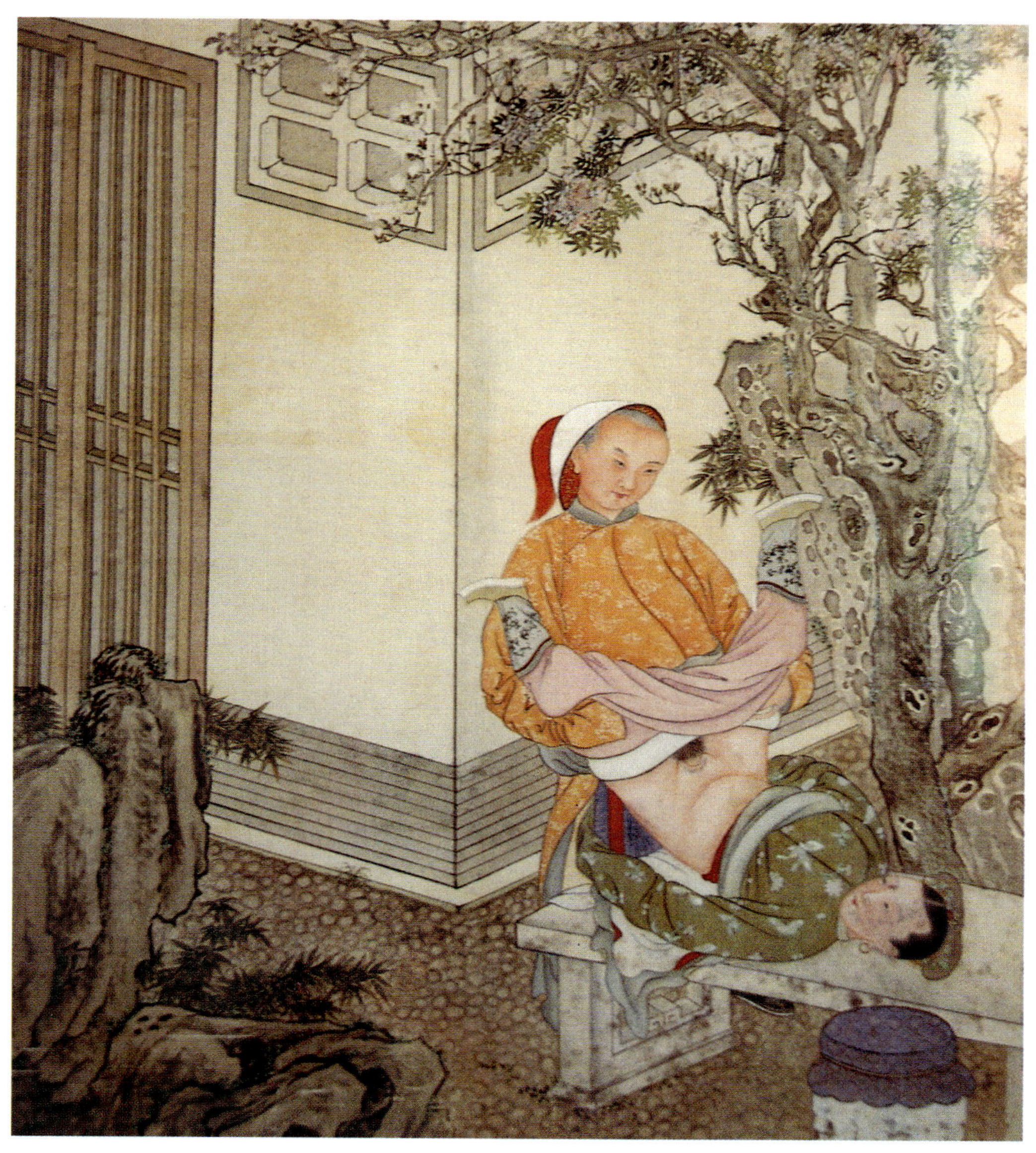

A Chinese nobleman robed in orange brocade is shown removing pink silk trousers from a lady who leans back on a bench. This beginning of the Taoist love posture known as *Soaring Sea Gulls* takes place in a garden under a tree, with craggy rocks at either side.

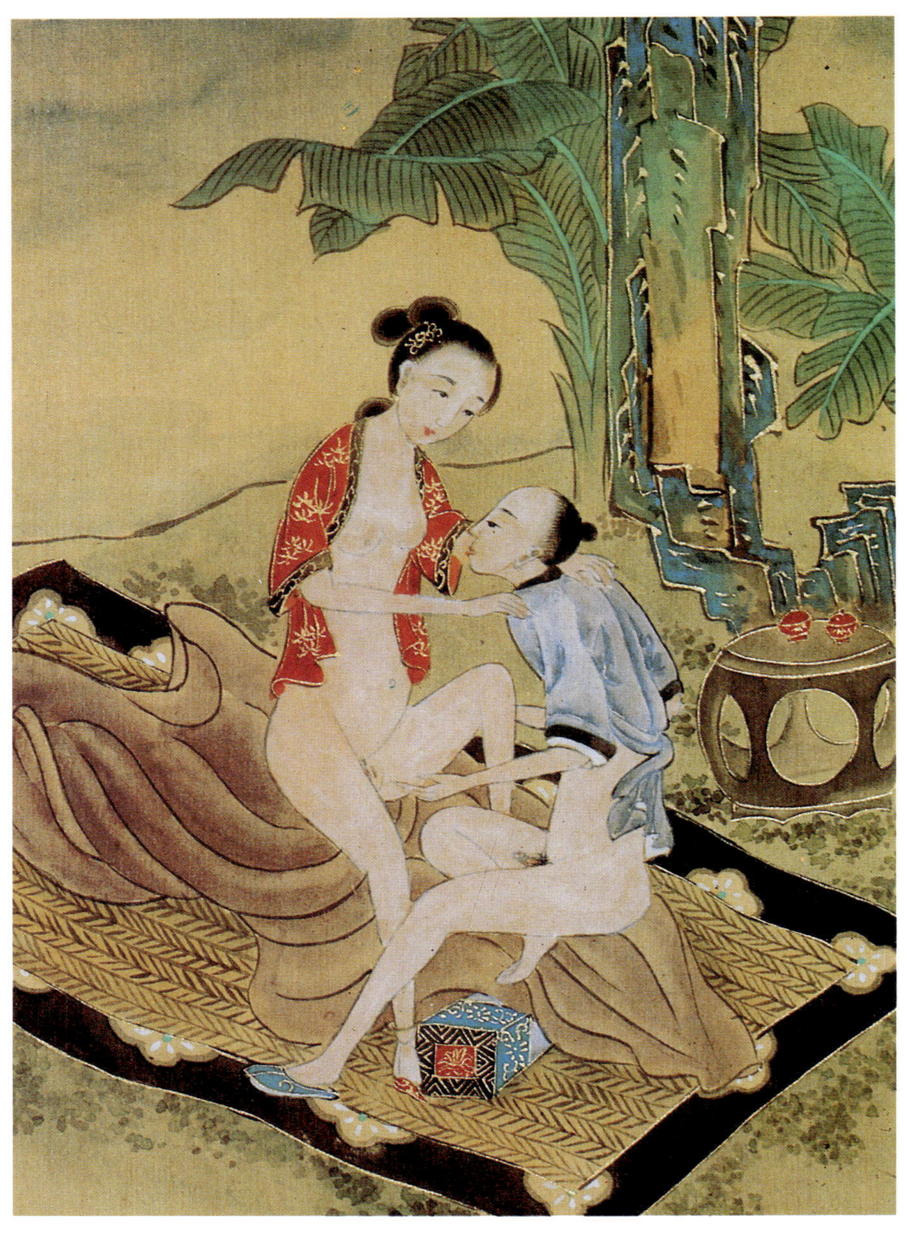

This fine Chinese album painting shows a couple engaged in foreplay upon a mat within a private garden. The man gazes longingly at his partner's breasts while reaching to caress her "Jade Gateway." Two teacups are placed close by, for refreshment. The banana grove beyond suggests the abundance of their love.

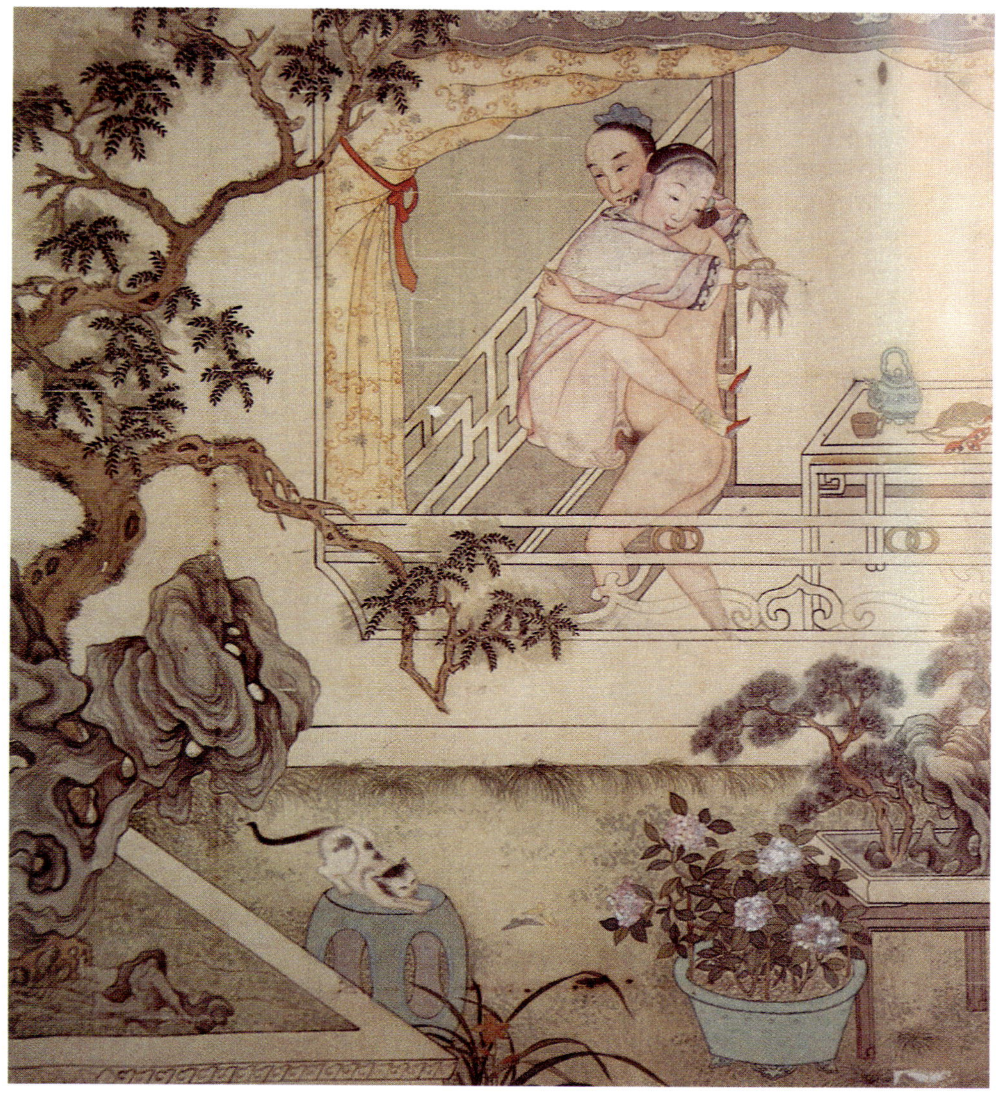

A Chinese couple are shown within a room viewed from a courtyard, in erotic union in a standing position related to the Bamboo Near the Altar posture. Supporting his pink-robed consort on a railing, the man submerges his "Positive Peak" into her "Inner Terrace." She drapes herself over her lover's shoulders, displaying her long fingernails. The trees, flowers, and stretching cat emphasize the Taoist ideal of harmonizing with Nature. The teapot and cups on the table suggest shared intimacy.

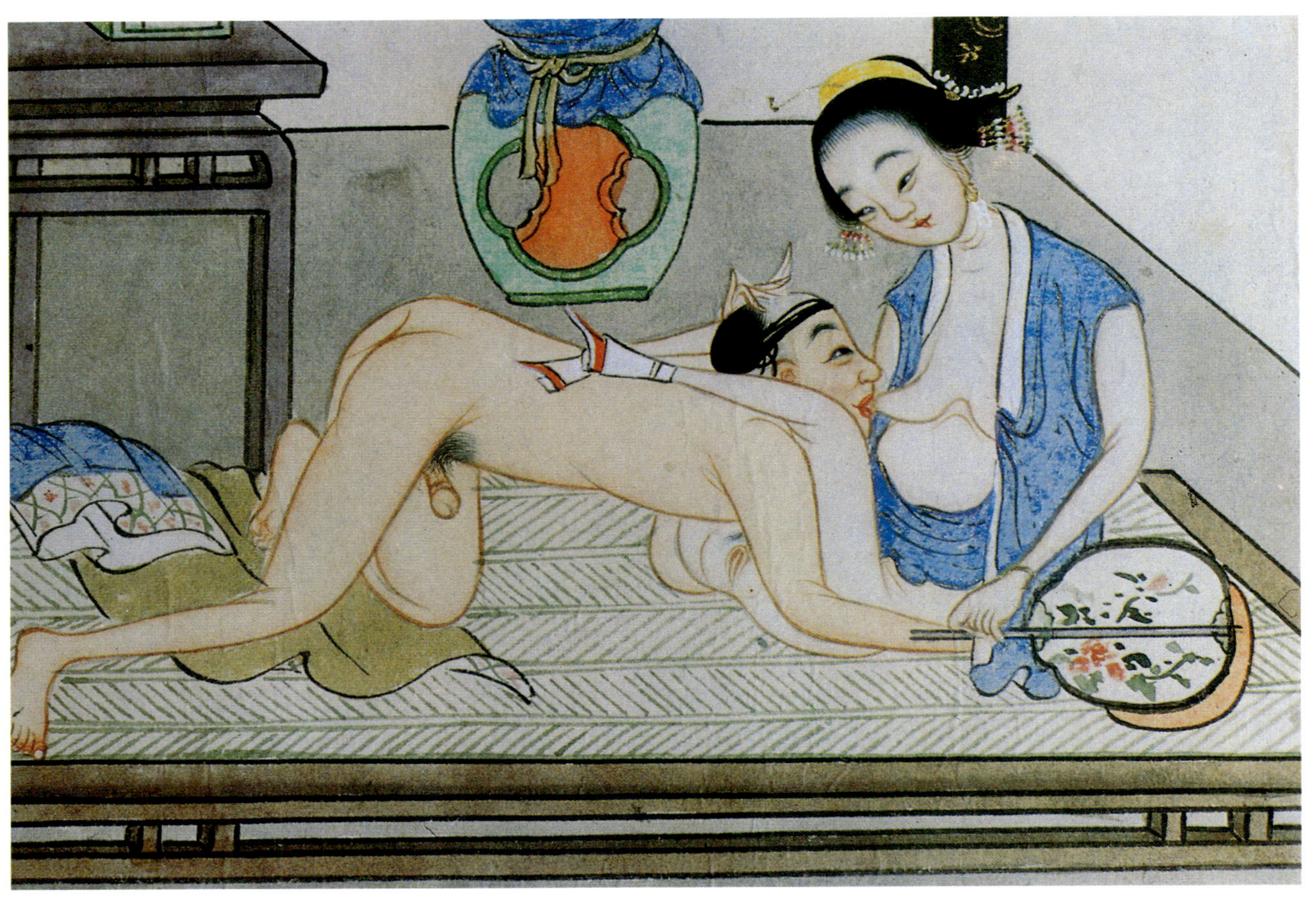

In a detail from a Chinese watercolor a man is shown kissing his partner's right breast while she wraps her legs around his neck and holds a fan in her left hand. Taoism teaches that a subtle vitalizing essence known as White Snow, Essence of Coral, or Immortality Peach Juice is produced from the breasts of a woman when she is sexually excited. The delicate colors of this composition convey a mood of tenderness.

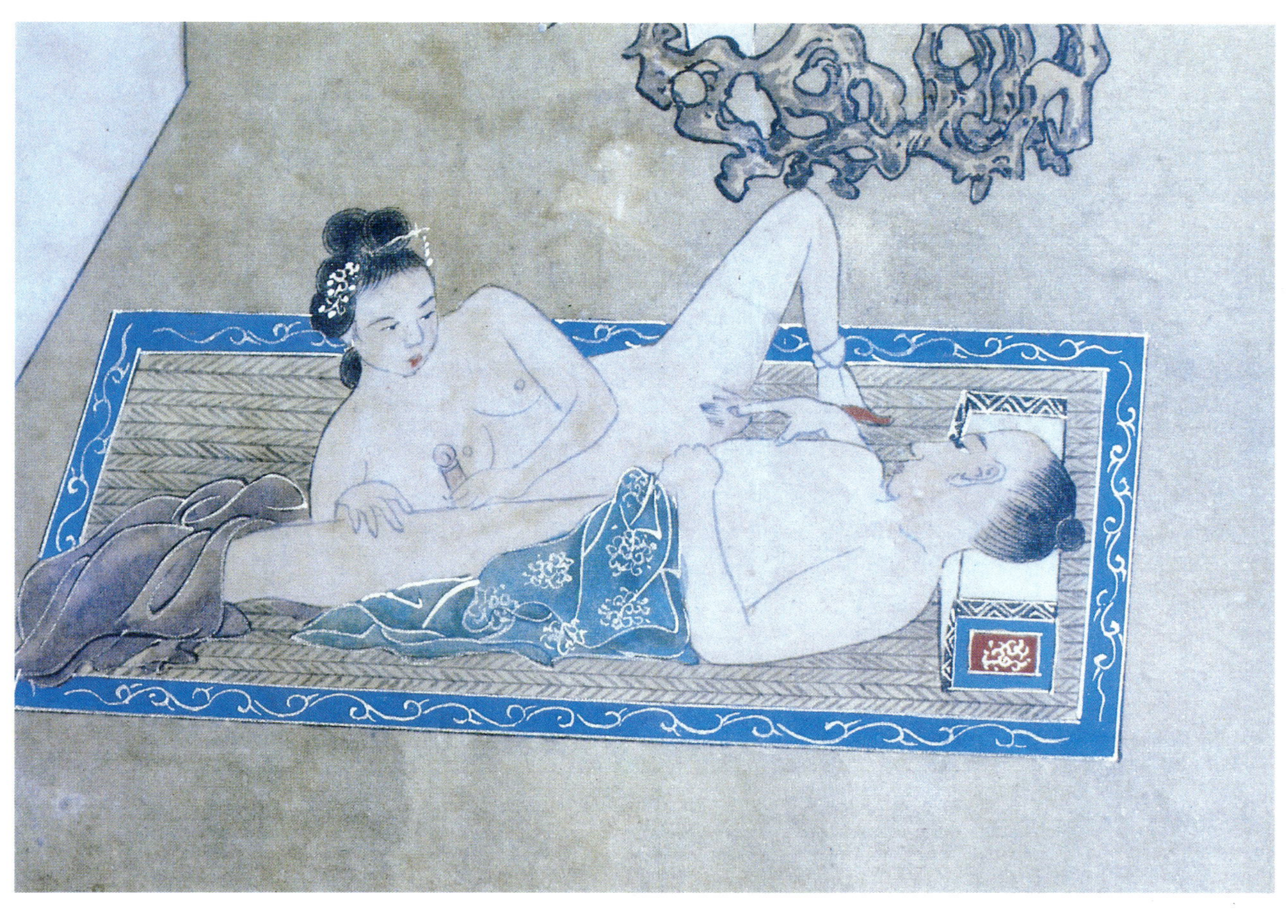

A Chinese couple are shown engaged in foreplay upon a mat. The woman firmly clasps her partner's "Ambassador" as she gazes at his face; he in turn gently opens the lips of her "Honey Pot." In this detail from a larger composition the mineral green and blue highlights contrast with the larger expanse of neutral tones as the crimson and gold details take on a jewellike quality.

Every time a man wishes to make love, there is a certain order of things to
be followed. In the first place the man should harmonize his mood with that
of the woman. Only then will his Jade Stalk rise.

Su-nu-ching

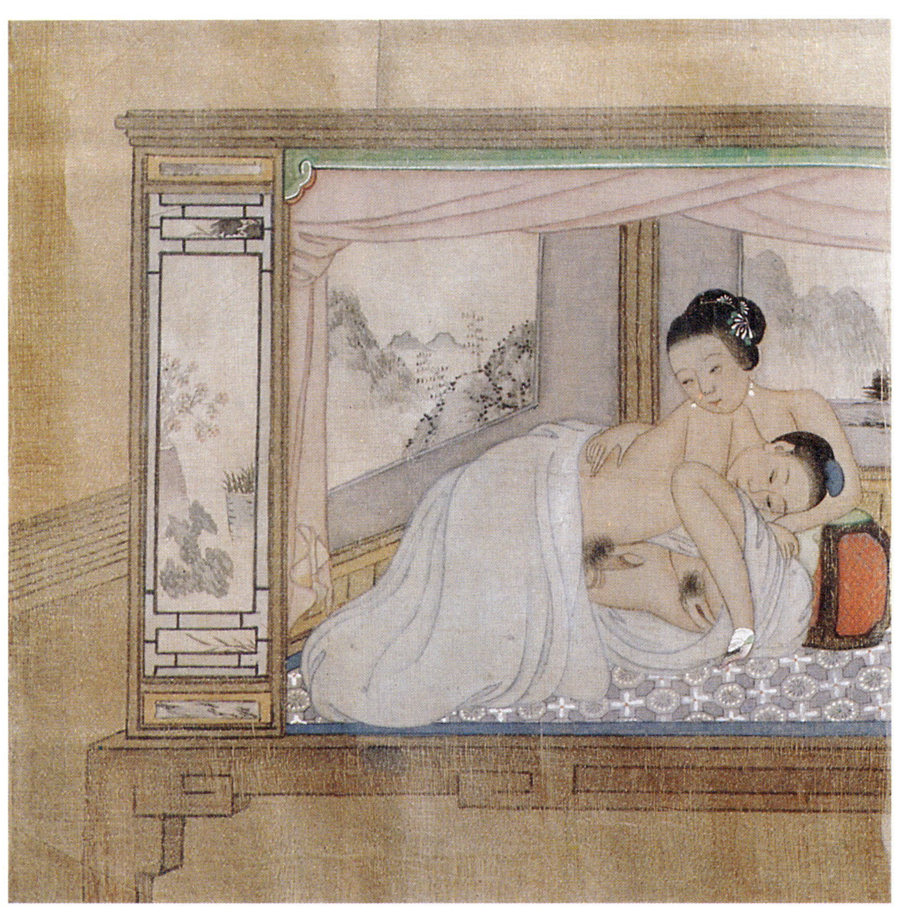

*A Chinese couple are shown preparing to make love on an ornate bed which is almost a room unto
itself. A mood of tenderness and love is expressed as the man leans over his partner's body, as if in
worship, before penetrating her "Love Grotto." Exquisite landscapes embellish the bed, adding an air of
naturalism.*

Their two hearts beat as one,
They pressed together fragrant shoulders
And touched each other's cheeks.
He grasped that perfumed breast,
Smooth as the softest down,
And found it perfect.

Chin P'ing Mei

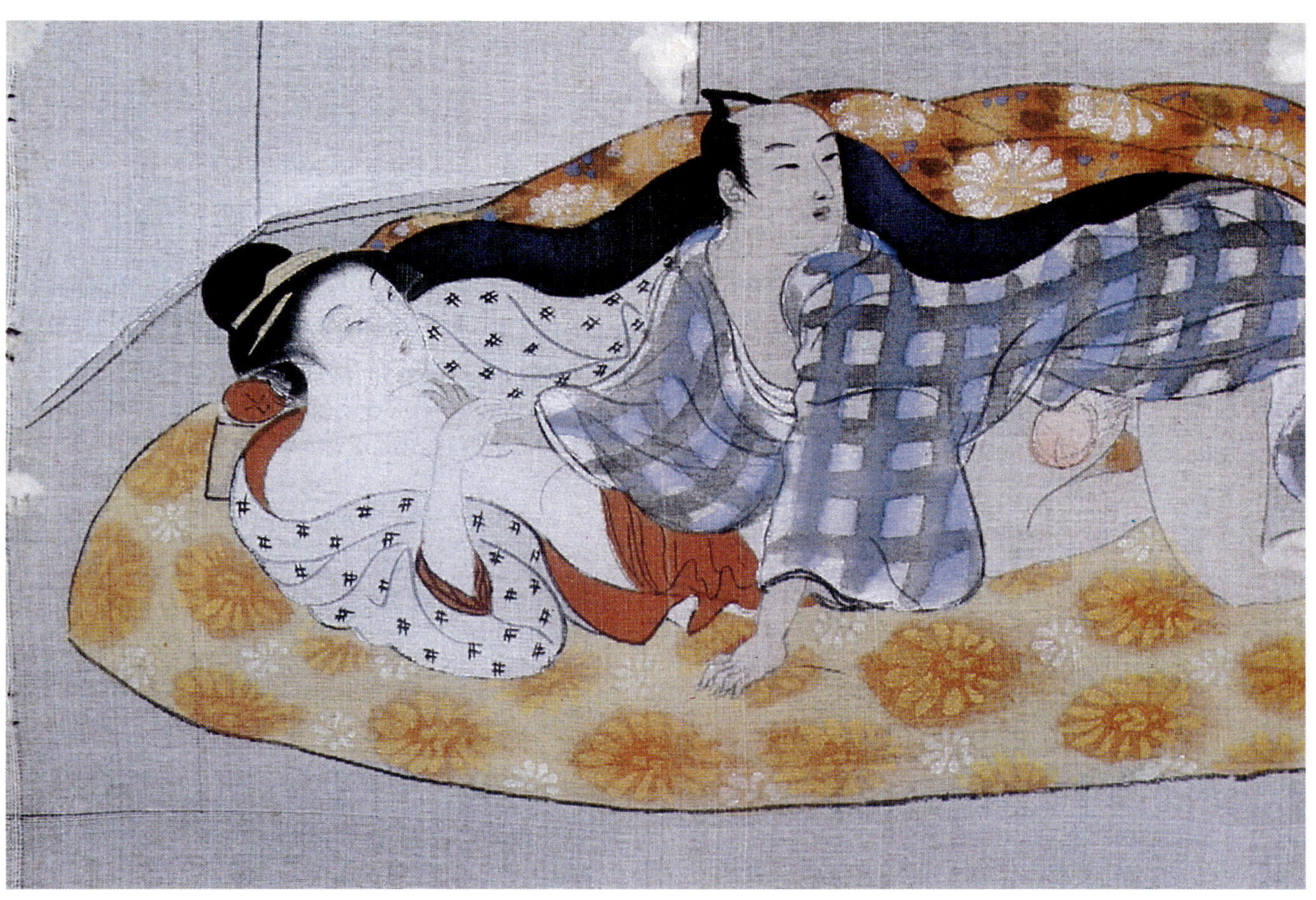

This Shunga painting shows a Japanese couple about to make love upon a futon mattress. His "Weapon of Love" ready for "battle," the man turns to look over his shoulder, perhaps at a sudden intruder who has disturbed their intimacy.

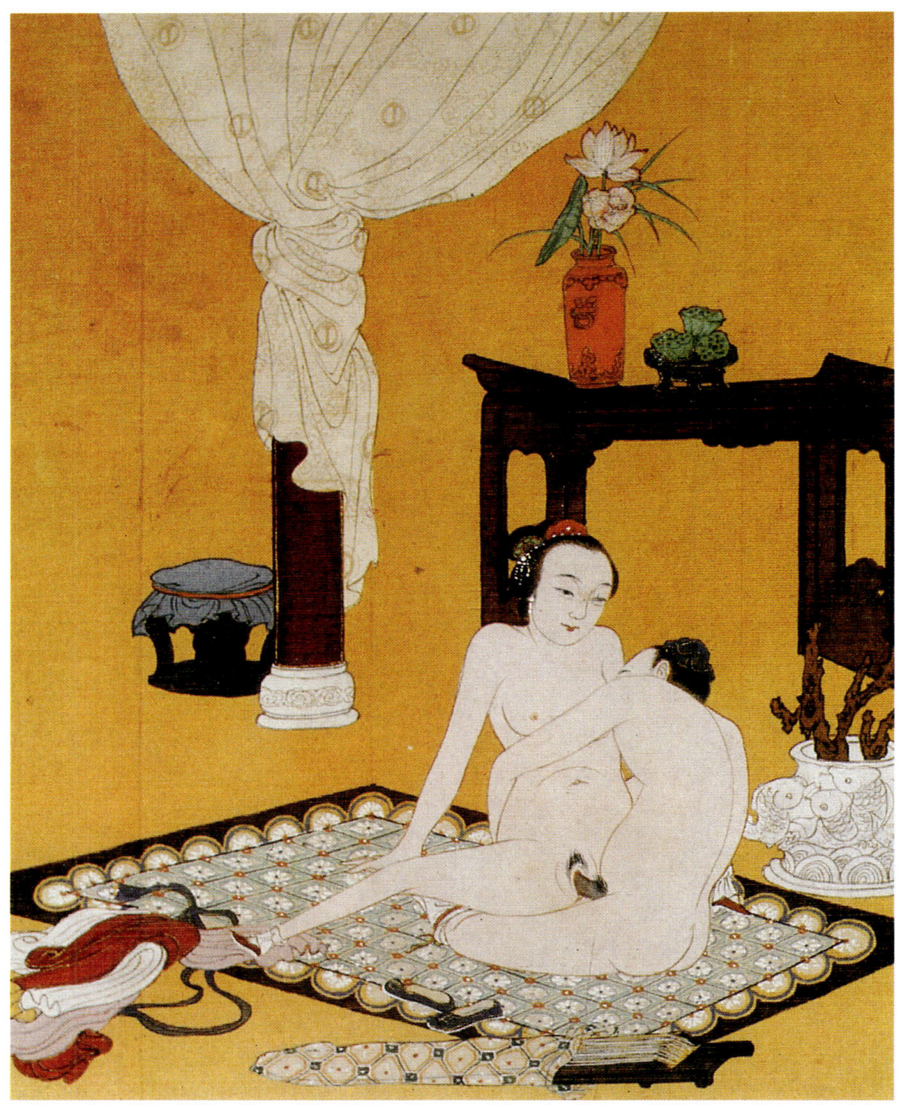

The "Positive Peak" has entered the "Pleasure Grotto." A Chinese couple sit in union upon an ornate mat while a pink lotus bursts open on a table behind them. As they perform the Taoist love posture known as Shouting Monkey Embracing a Tree, the man sucks his lover's left breast while she gazes at him serenely. To one side a fish-motif pot contains a bonzai miniature tree, the pot symbolic of sexual energy and the tree of longevity.

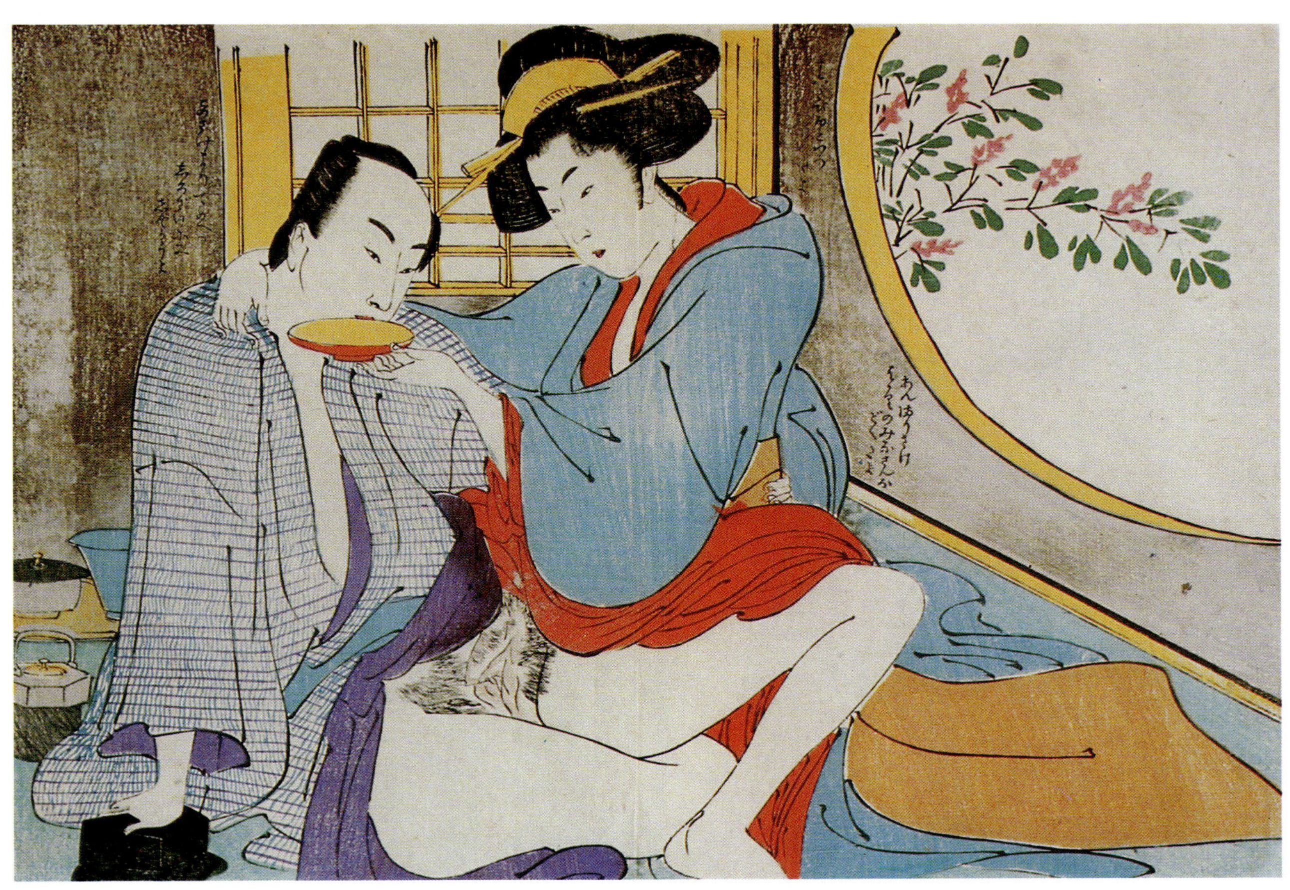

This *Shunga* print shows a Japanese couple in a version of the classical Shouting Monkey posture. The woman raises up a cup of wine to her lover's lips while seated in union upon him; she personifies the Geisha spirit of service and active eroticism. The lively mixture of warm and cool colors enhances the play between active and passive roles.

Suddenly he lunged and reached the innermost Citadel; for within the Gate of Womanhood there is a Citadel, like the heart of a flower, which if touched by the Conqueror, is infused with wonderful pleasure.

Chin P'ing Mei

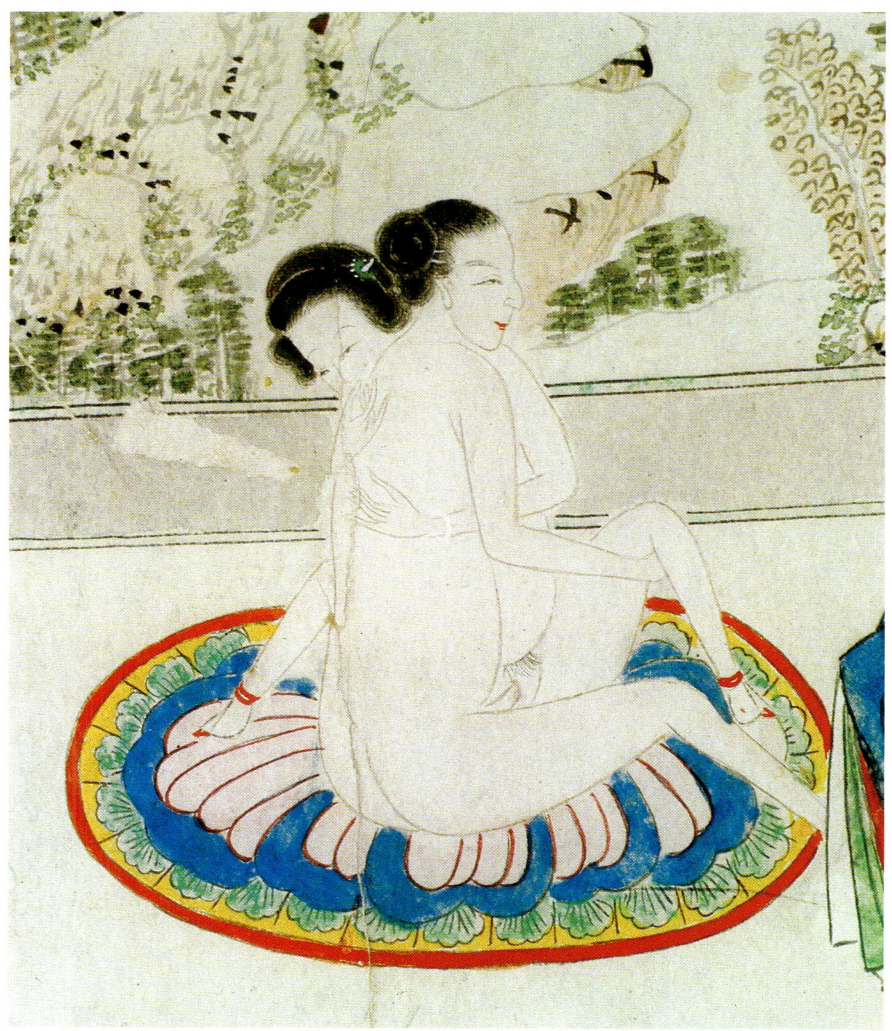

Here a Chinese couple are shown seated in union upon a brightly colored circular mat within the confines of a house. They make love in the Taoist All-Encompassing posture, devised to prolong ecstacy and enhance the mutual absorption of love essences; behind them a large painted screen displays scenes of nature.

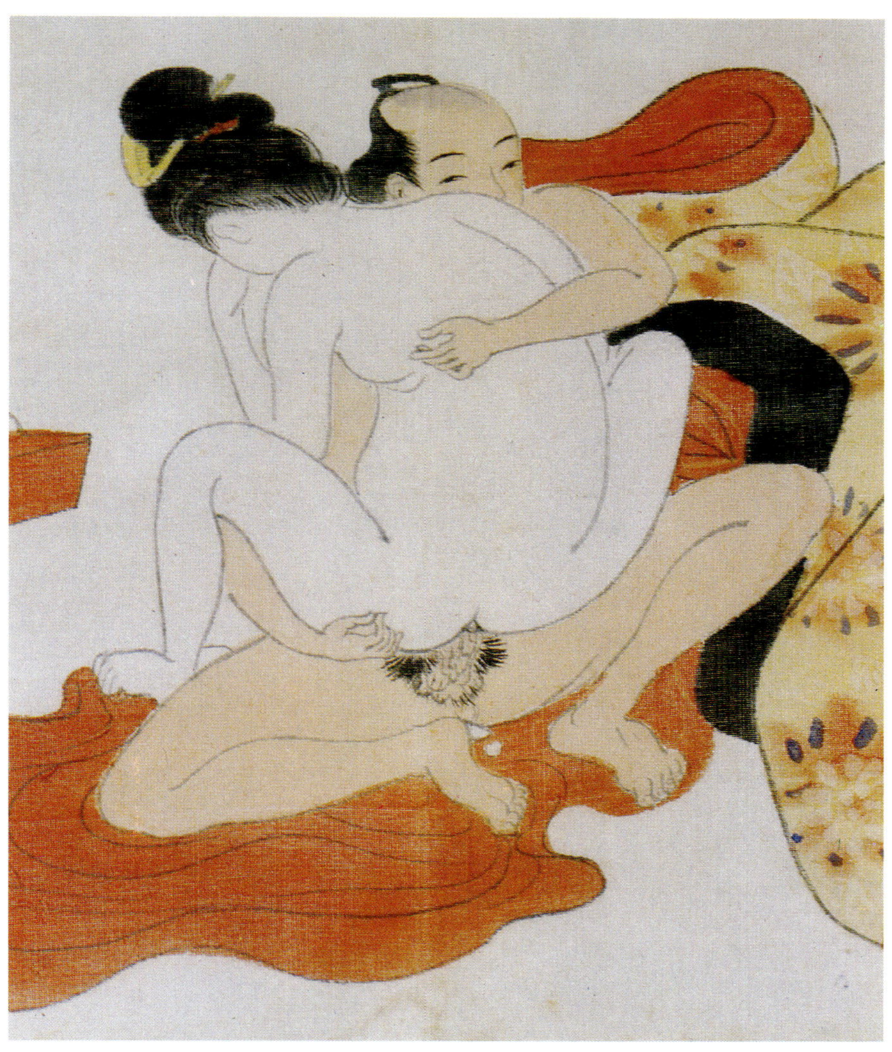

A Japanese couple are seated in close union in the classical posture known as Cranes with Joined Necks. The pale translucent skin of the woman's back forms the central focus of this composition of gracefully flowing lines and natural earth colors.

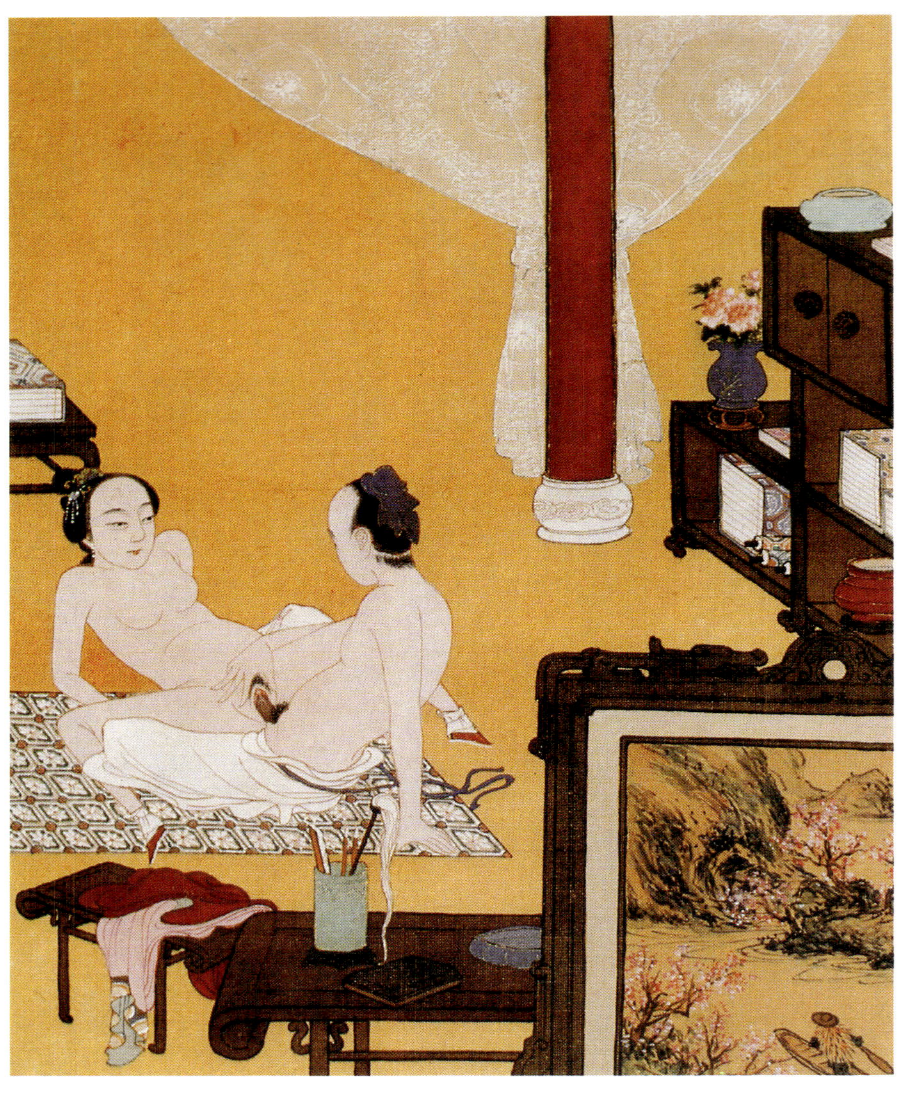

A Chinese couple make love in seated union upon a mat within a room. The diaphanous drapes and fine furniture and fittings seem to reflect the pink hue of the lovers' naked skin. As his partner leans back, the man presses his right hand around her "Golden Furrow" to aid control over ejaculation; this is a variation of the classical Taoist love posture known as Fluttering Phoenix. The blossoms on the screen and in a vase on the table suggest renewal.

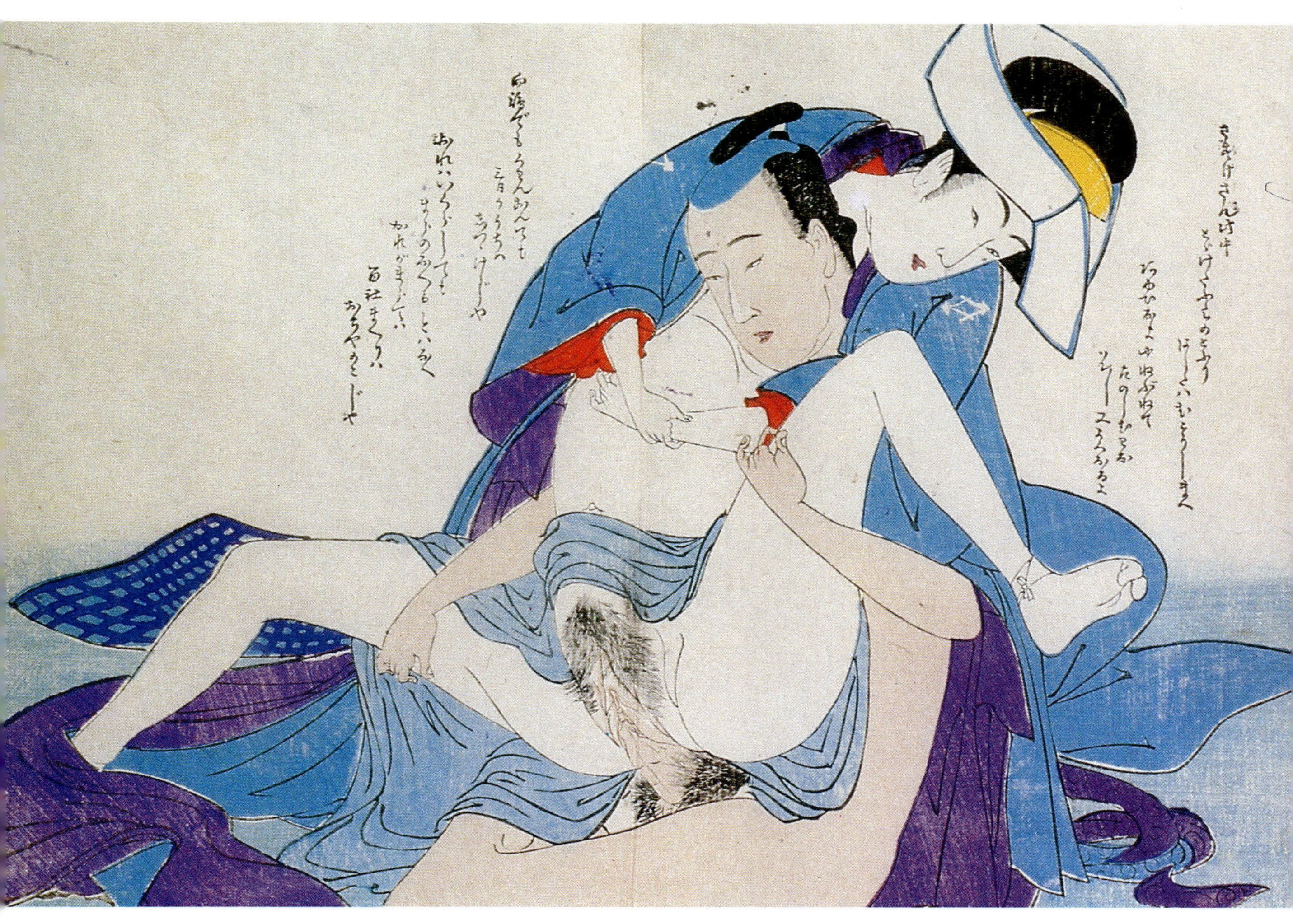

The woman is shown seated with her back to her partner in the Taoist love posture known as Mountain Goat Facing a Tree. The blues and purples of this Shunga print from Japan convey a mood of mystic eroticism, heightened by the wild abandon of the couple.

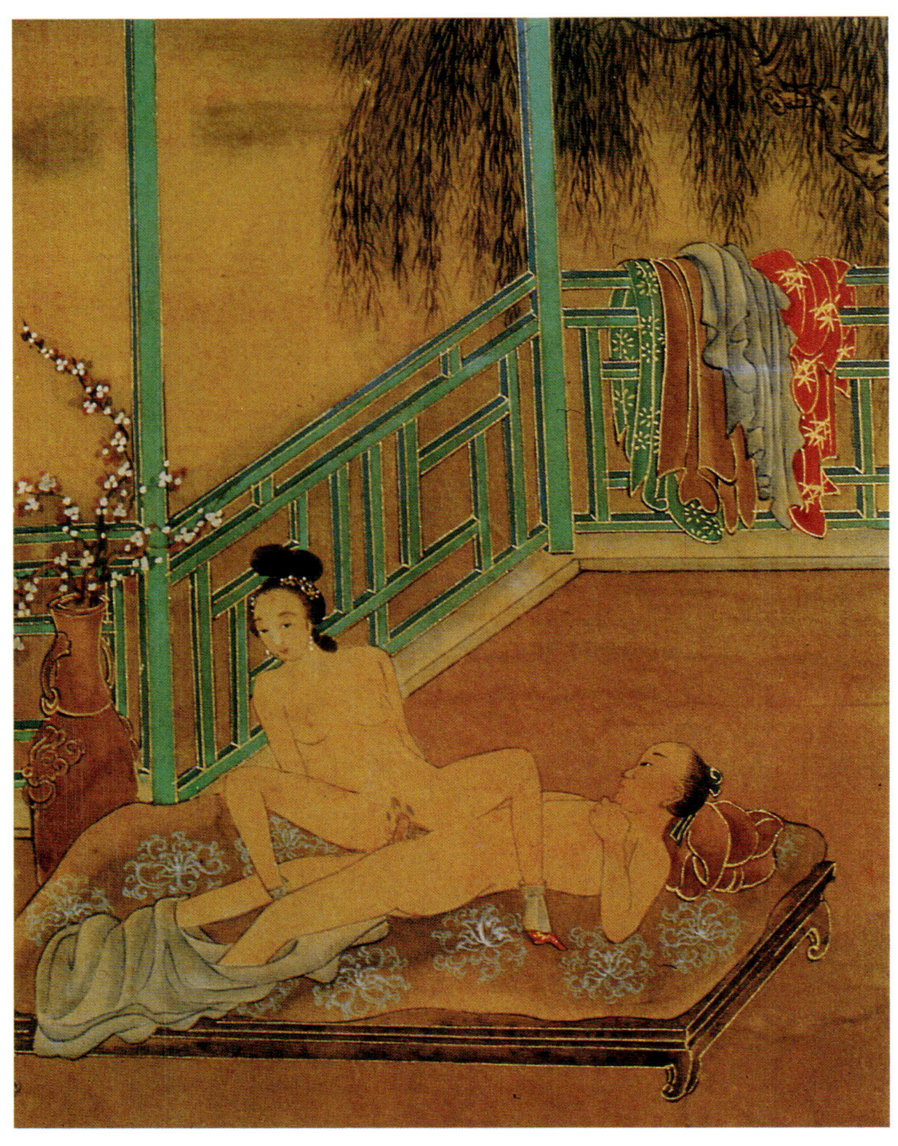

A Chinese couple are shown in union upon a bed placed on a veranda. Their discarded garments hang over a railing, behind which a willow tree, symbolic of constancy, can be seen. The couple are performing a secret Taoist therapeutic love posture in which the woman is dominant while the man retains. The vase of blossoms by their side suggests renewal.

Spring has come and the flowers are brilliant with color;
Responding to the rhythms of love, your supple body moves.
Opening, opening is that most Precious Bud;
My drops of dew help your Peony bloom.

Chang Sheng

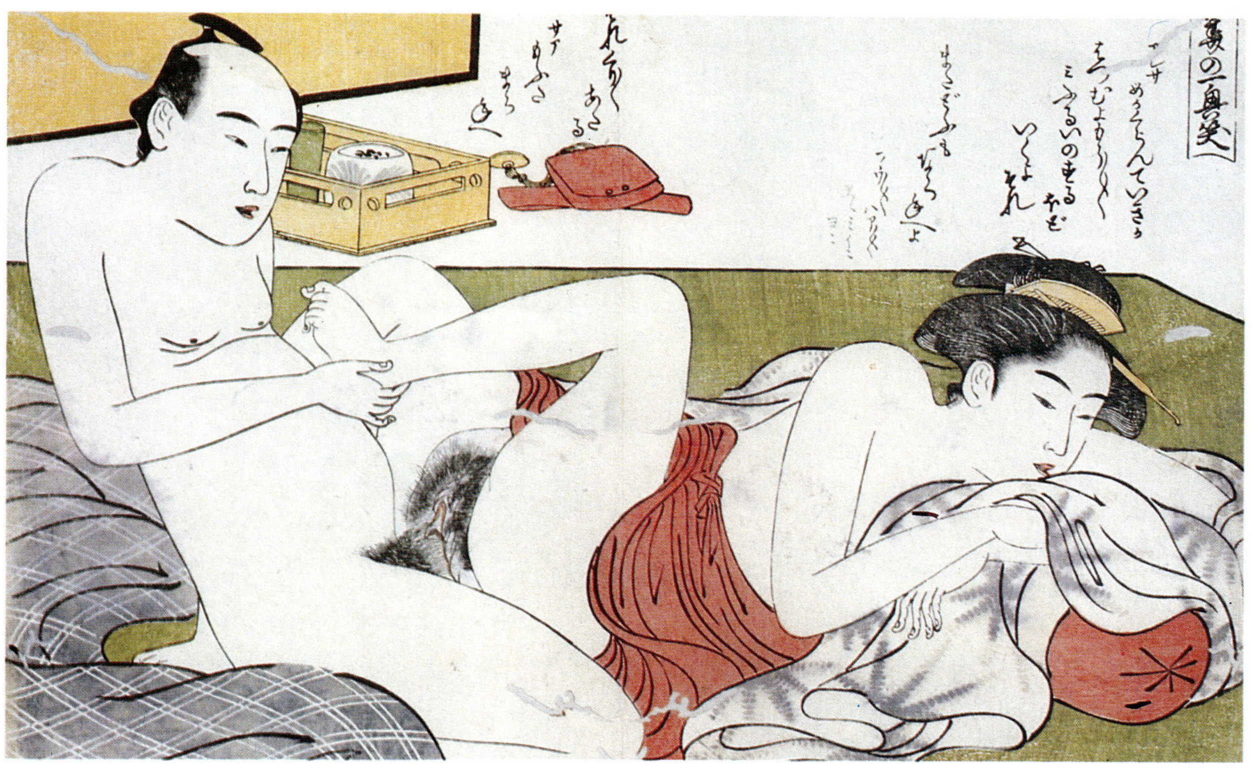

This fine Japanese print depicts a couple in union in the Pawing Horse posture, the man artfully raising his partner's leg while she leans upon a pillow. Love-cloths are scattered in the foreground.

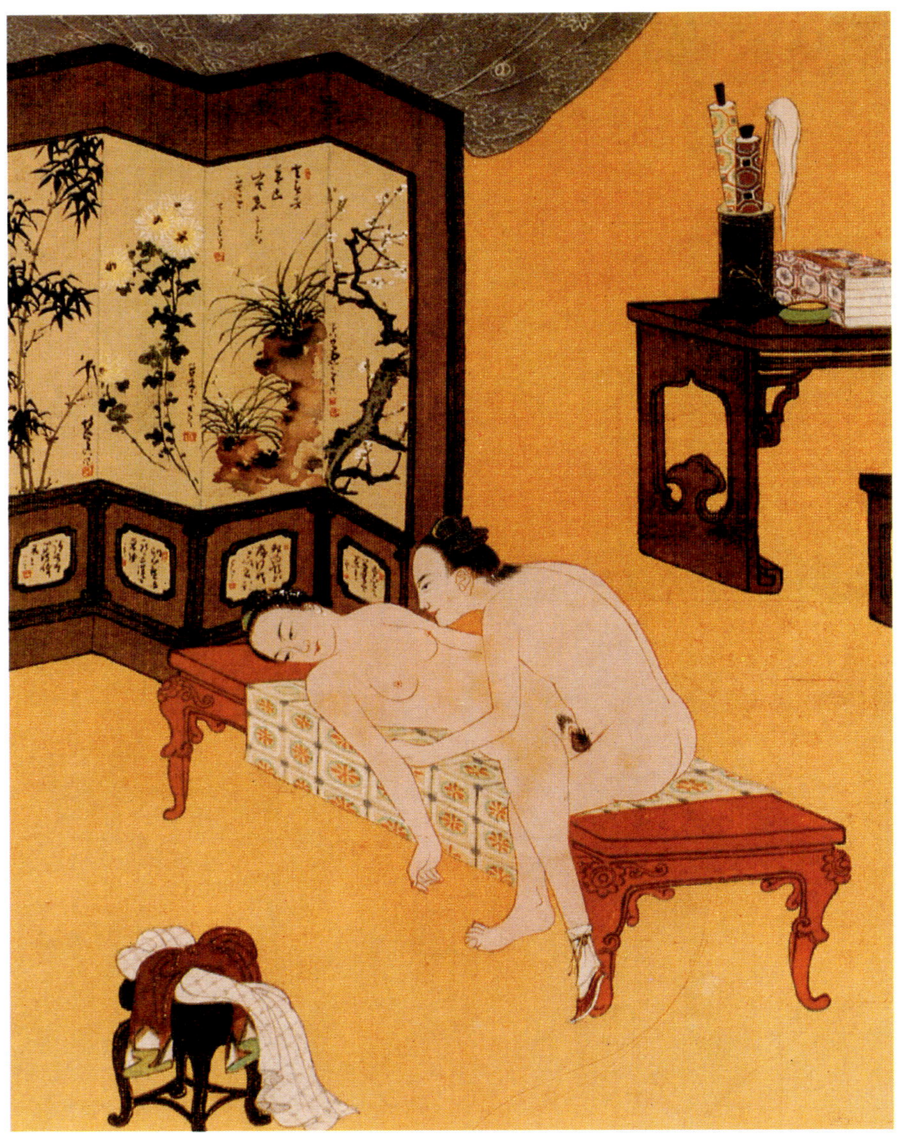

A Chinese couple make love upon a red lacquer bed behind an exquisite folding screen decorated with studies from nature. The woman leans back suggestively in the posture known as *Pair of Swallows,* turning her head to one side. A feeling of intensity is suggested by the red colors contrasting against the pale skin and yellow silk background.

Shedding my robes and removing my makeup,
I roll out the picture-scroll by the pillow's side;
Acting as an Initiatress into the Arts of Love,
We perfect the postures and taste those rare delights.
  Chang Heng's poem of a bride to her husband

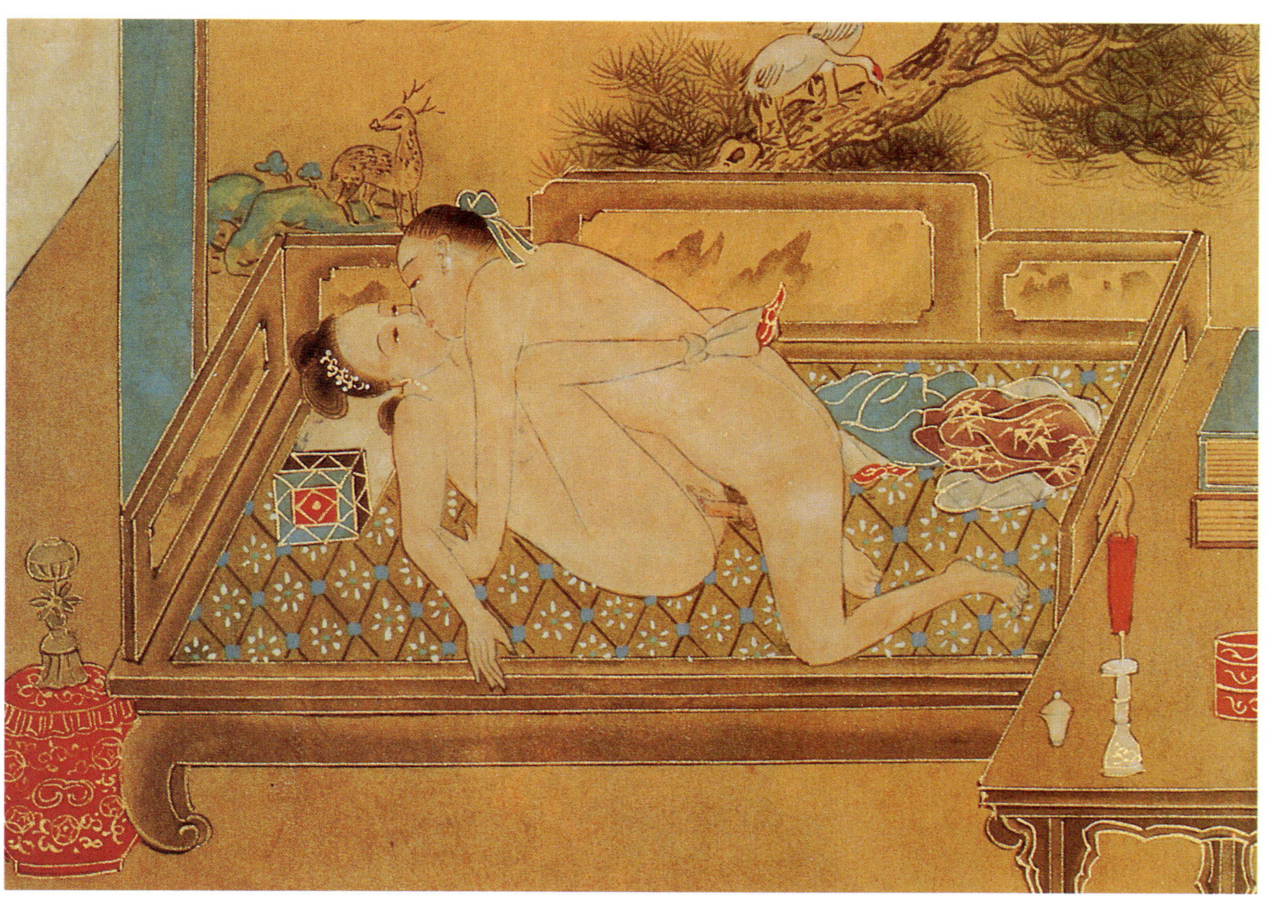

Passion develops as a Chinese couple make love in the Fluttering Phoenix posture upon a couch. A nearby table holds two pillow books and a burning red candle, suggestive of the fires of passion. On a screen behind the couple are painted a pair of cranes, symbolizing fidelity, and an antlered deer, the glyph of virility. The use of gold to outline the forms of the composition adds a spiritual quality.

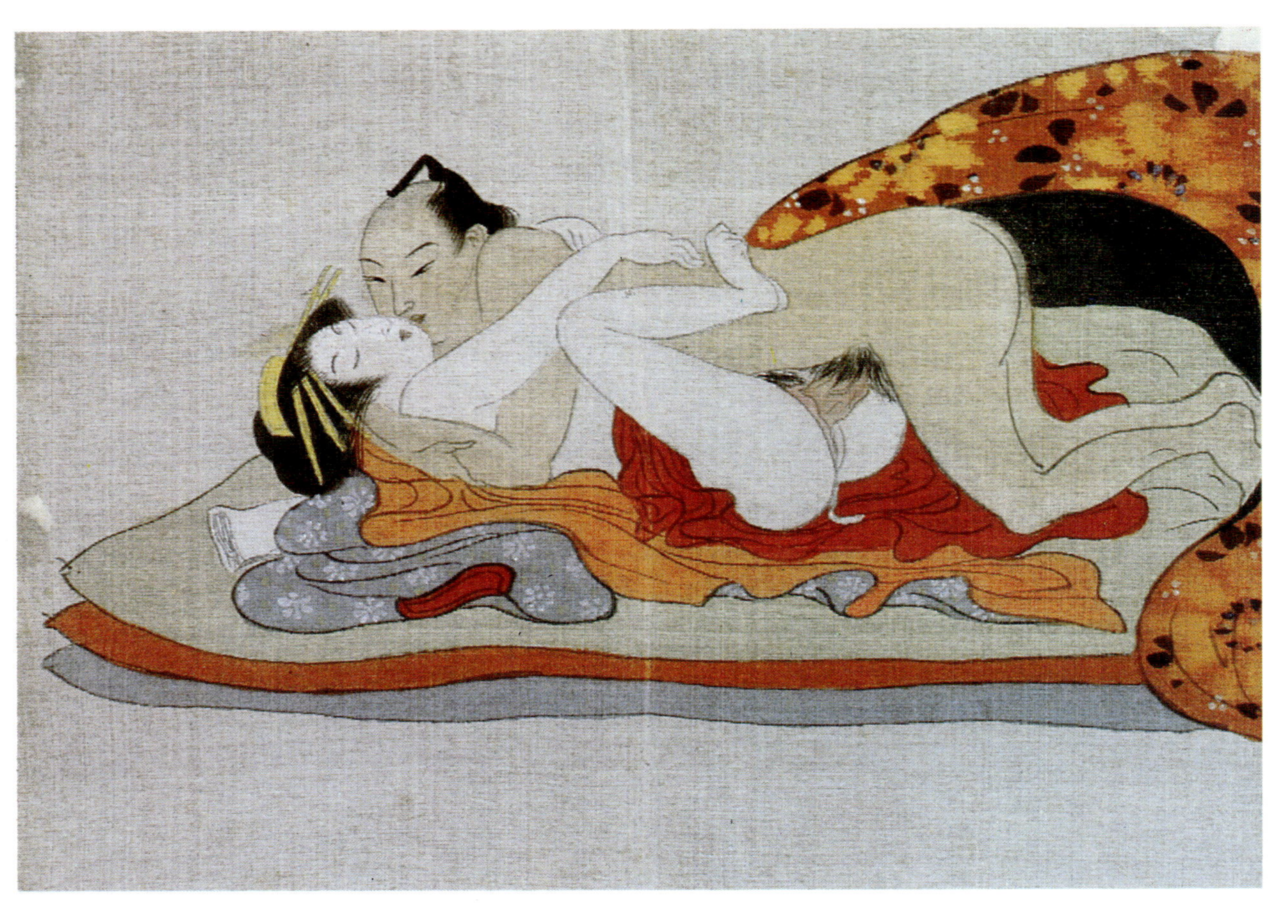

This Shunga painting shows a Japanese couple performing the Turning Dragon love posture. Love-juices are shown flowing outward from the "Mysterious Cavern" of the woman, who clasps her partner. The darker skin tone of the man emphasizes the alabaster whiteness of the woman's body as her toes curl in ecstasy.

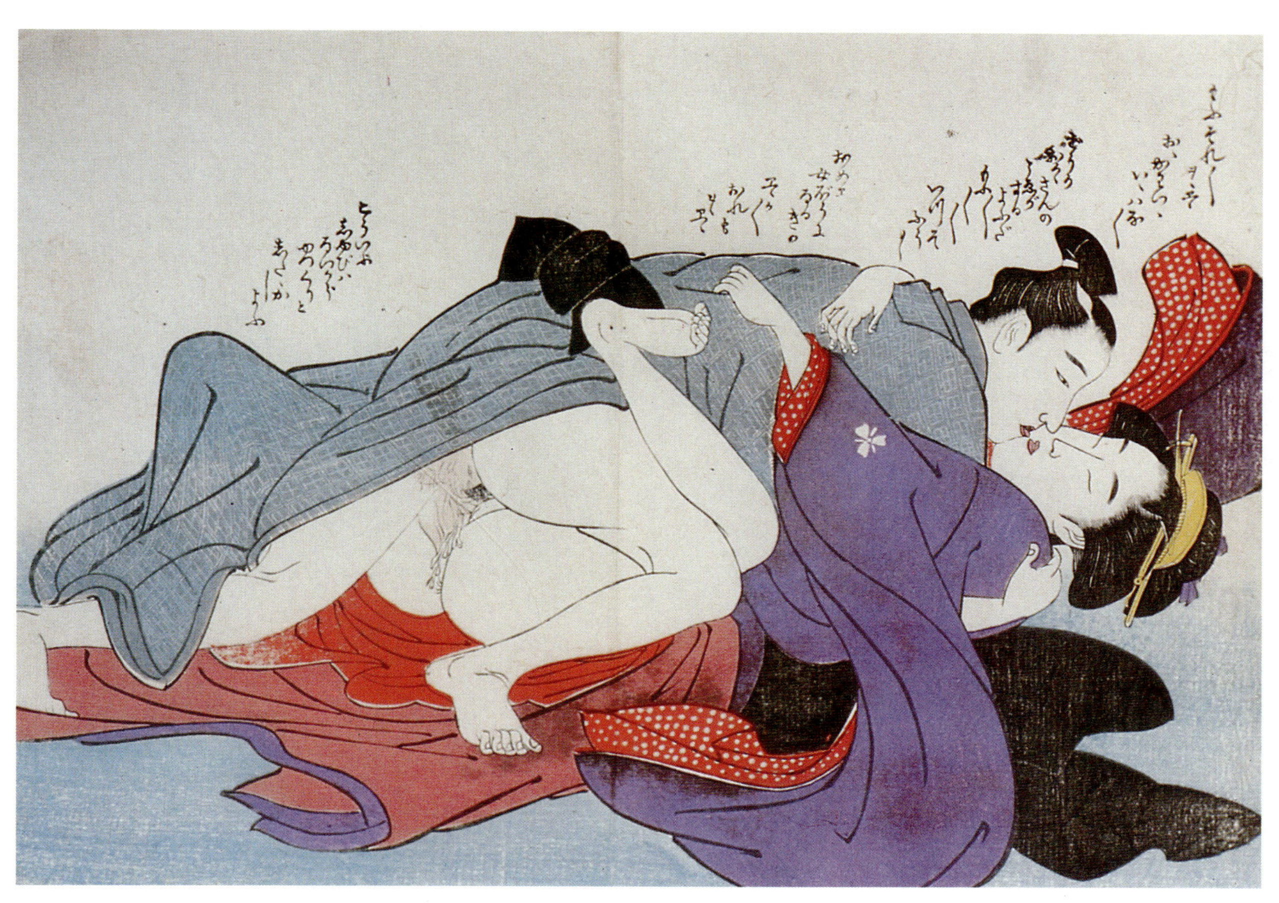

This fine Shunga print depicts a Japanese couple performing a variation of the Turning Dragon posture upon the floor in a moment of pure spontaneity. Love-juices flow copiously from the woman's "Pleasure Portal." The purple and red colors dominant in this composition aid the vivid expression of dynamic eroticism.

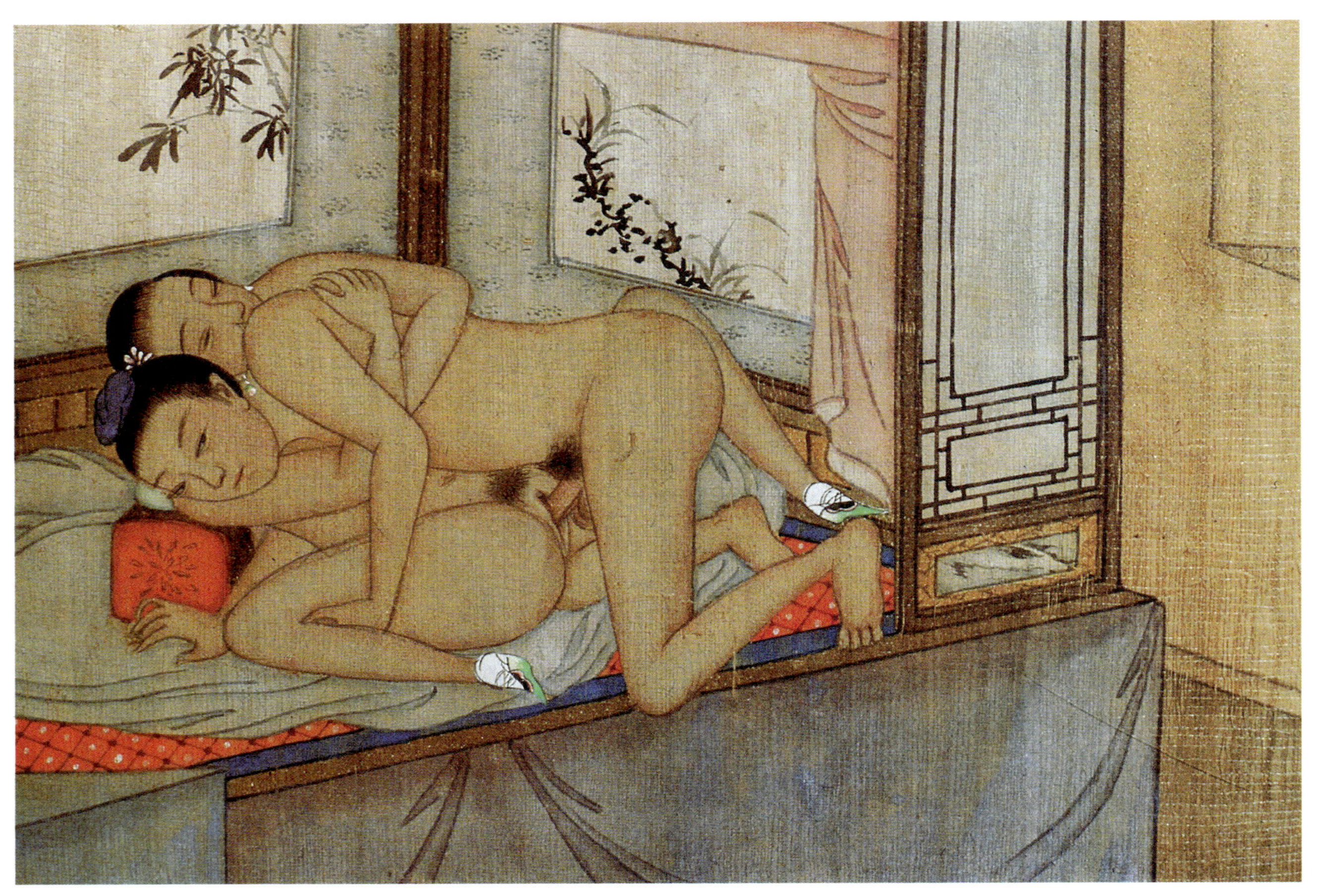

We slip beneath the silken covers,
All warm and scented; our moment comes,
The dew falls, the Precious Flower opens
In the tenderness of love; the Clouds
and the Rain complete us, complete us.
Huang Ching

A Chinese couple perform the "Mysteries of the Clouds and Rain" upon a beautiful bed ornamented with fine silks and naturalistic paintings. The woman ardently clasps her lover to her body as he spreads her thighs wide and moves his "Yang Pagoda" in and out of her "Secret Cavern."

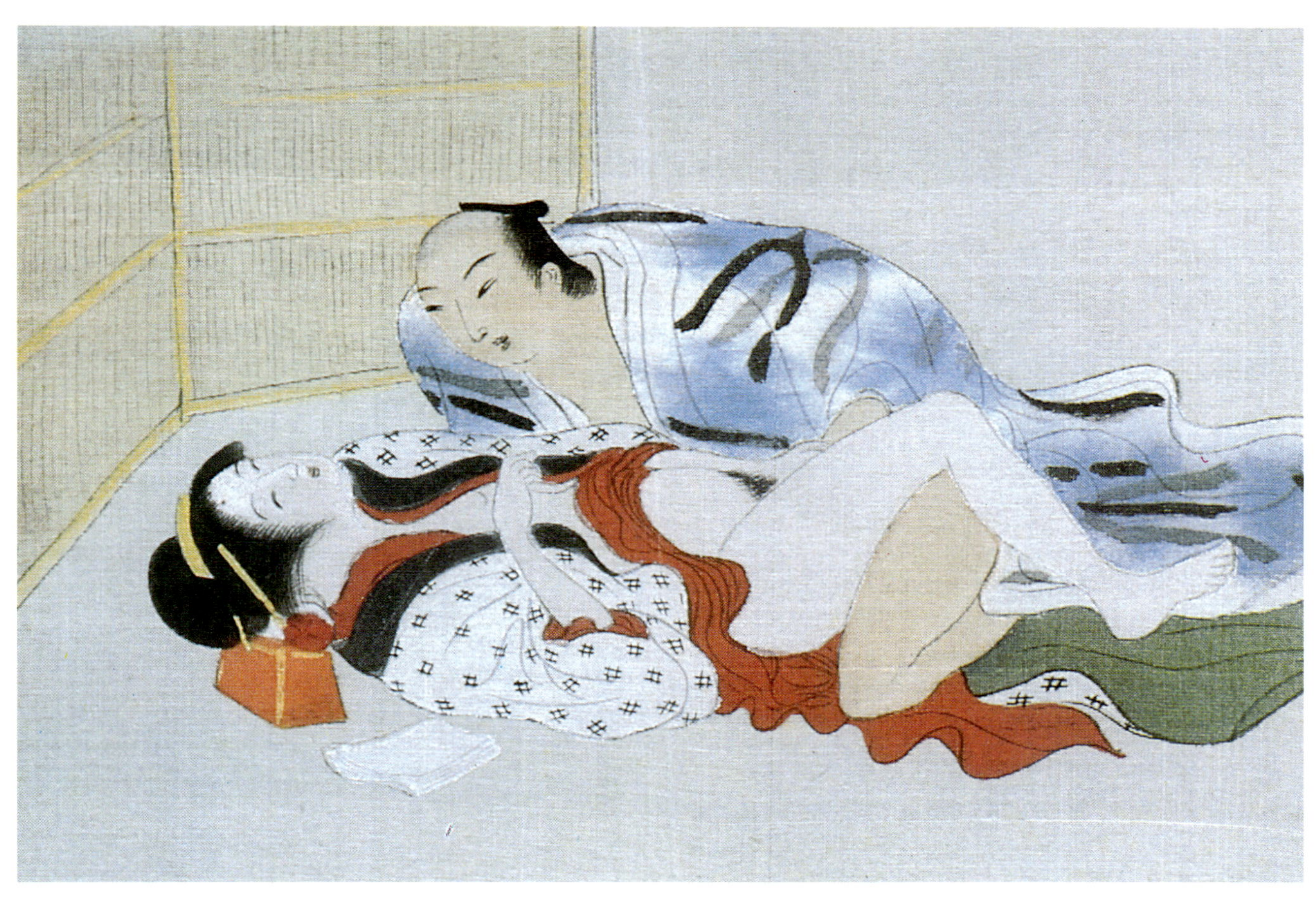

This Shunga painting depicts a partly clothed Japanese couple making love upon the floor in the Taoist posture known as *Pair of Swallows*. The woman lies back, her head resting on a hard pillow and her eyes closed; the man leans over and reaches for her *"Valley of Joy."* A mood of timelessness is created by the combination of color and line.

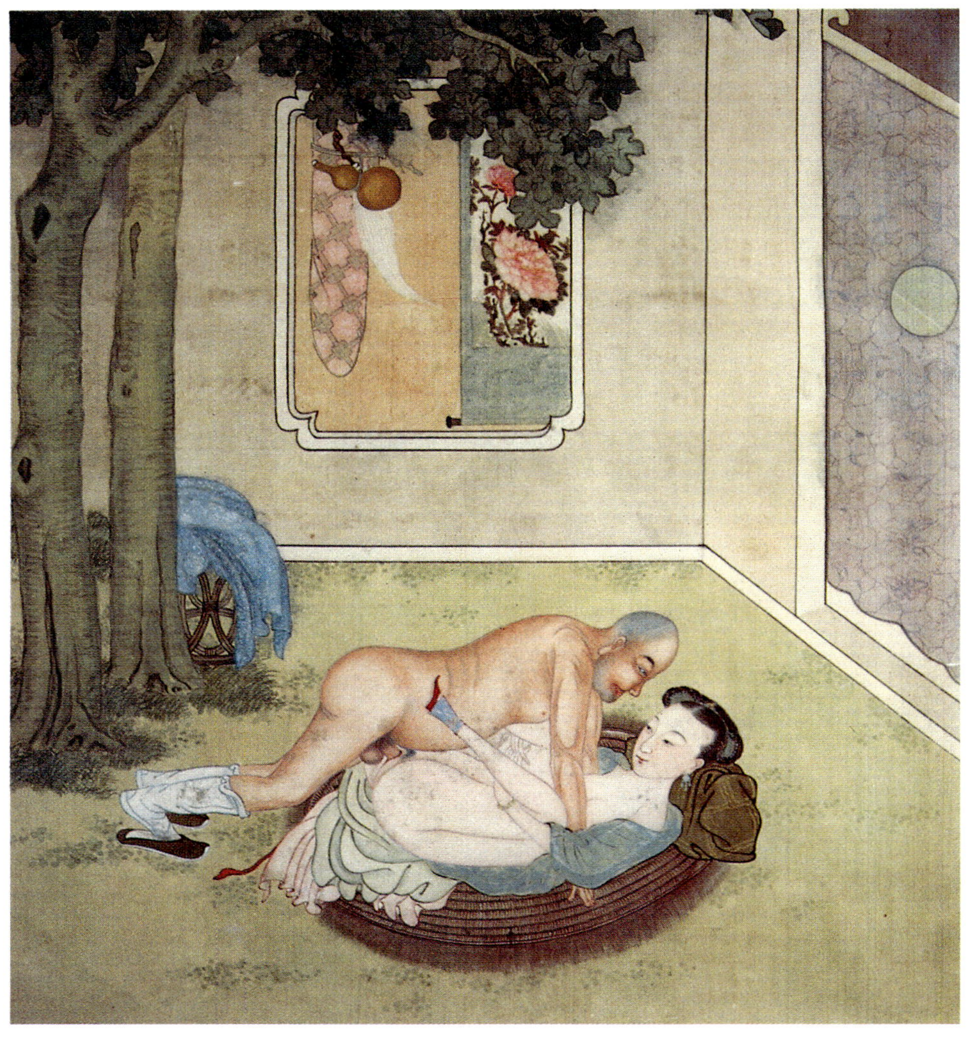

A naked elderly Chinese man makes love to a young lady in the posture known as Fluttering Phoenix, supporting himself on his outstretched arms. The woman lies back on a circular mat. Her white skin contrasts with the red shoes on her tiny "lotus feet." A double gourd hanging from a tree evokes the idea of Taoist alchemical vessels. This particular Taoist posture is practiced while retaining the semen and is said to cure the "hundred ailments."

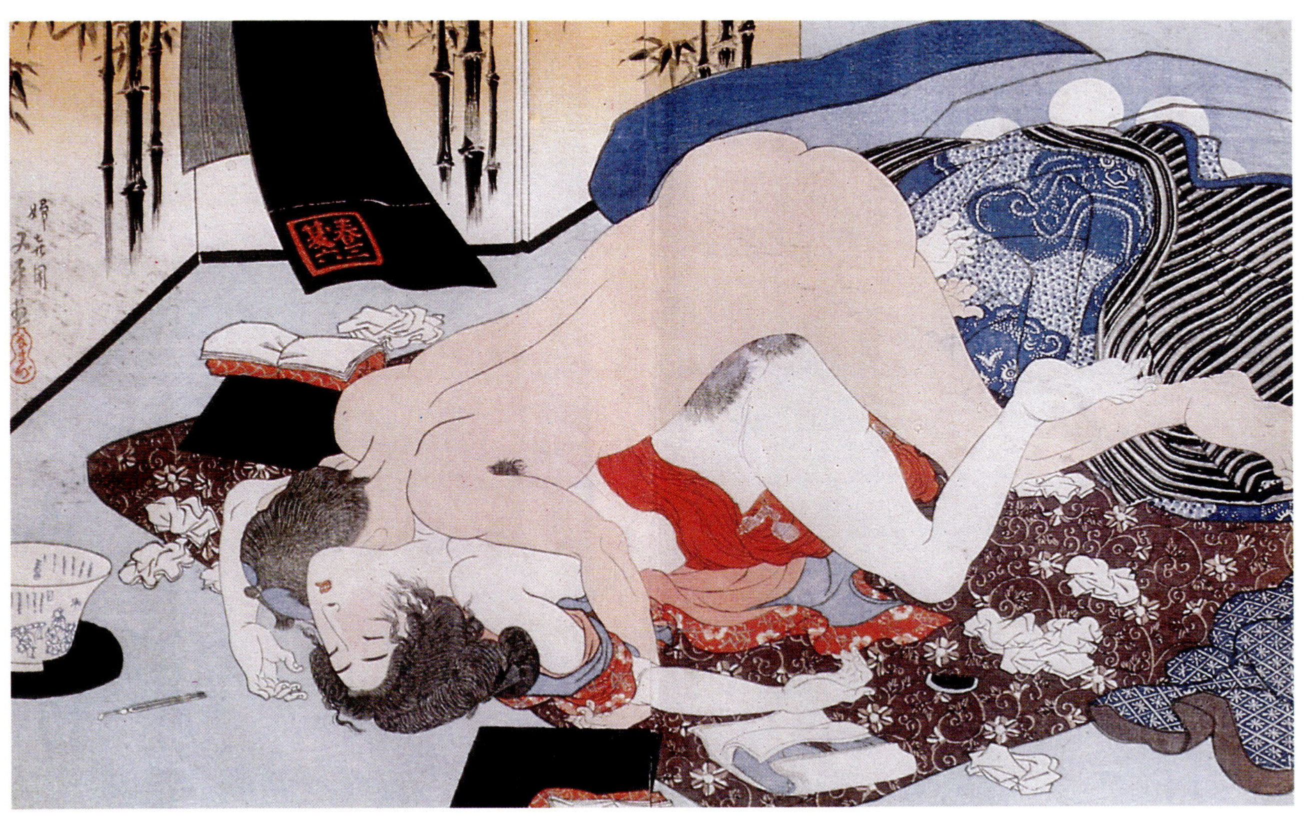

In this extraordinarily powerful Shunga print a Japanese couple are shown making love in absolute abandon. In their passion they have fallen from the bed. The woman's hair is disheveled and her thighs are wide apart as she raises up her "Pleasure House" to accommodate the busy thrusts of her partner's "Ambassador." Love-cloths lie scattered on the floor, suggesting climaxes already past.

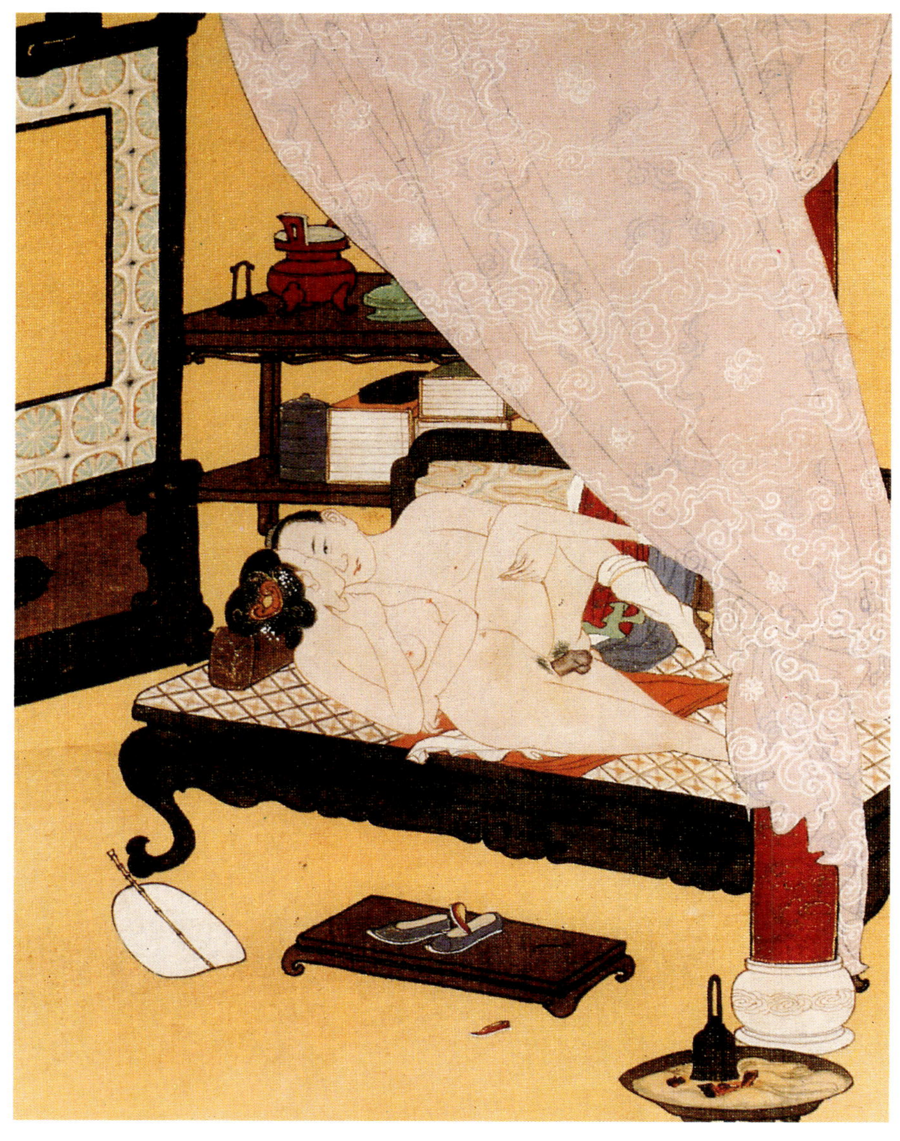

A Chinese couple recline on a bed, gazing into each other's eyes; it seems they are moving from one position to another. As the man carefully inserts his "Jade Stalk" into the "Cinnabar Crevice," the couple move into the Taoist posture known as Mandarin Ducks. The pale lilac drapes cling suggestively to a crimson column as a kettle rests on a bed of embers, ready for refreshment once the "Battle of Love" has taken its course.

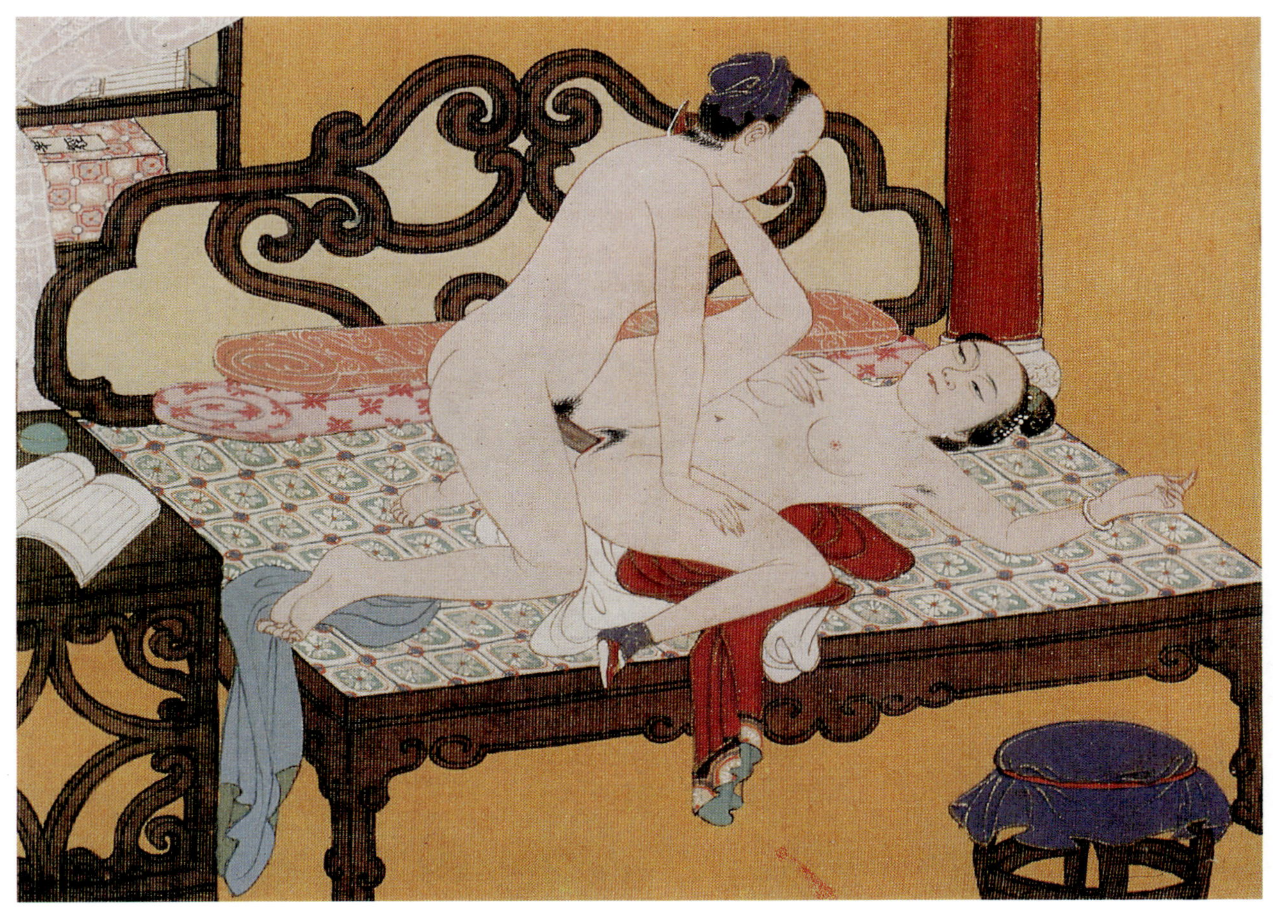

In this detail from a Chinese painting, a couple make love upon a carved bed. As the woman lies back and holds her left hand in a mystic gesture used for controlling and channeling sexual energy, the man leans over her, inserts his "Jade Stalk," and moves into the classic Taoist posture known as Pawing Horse.

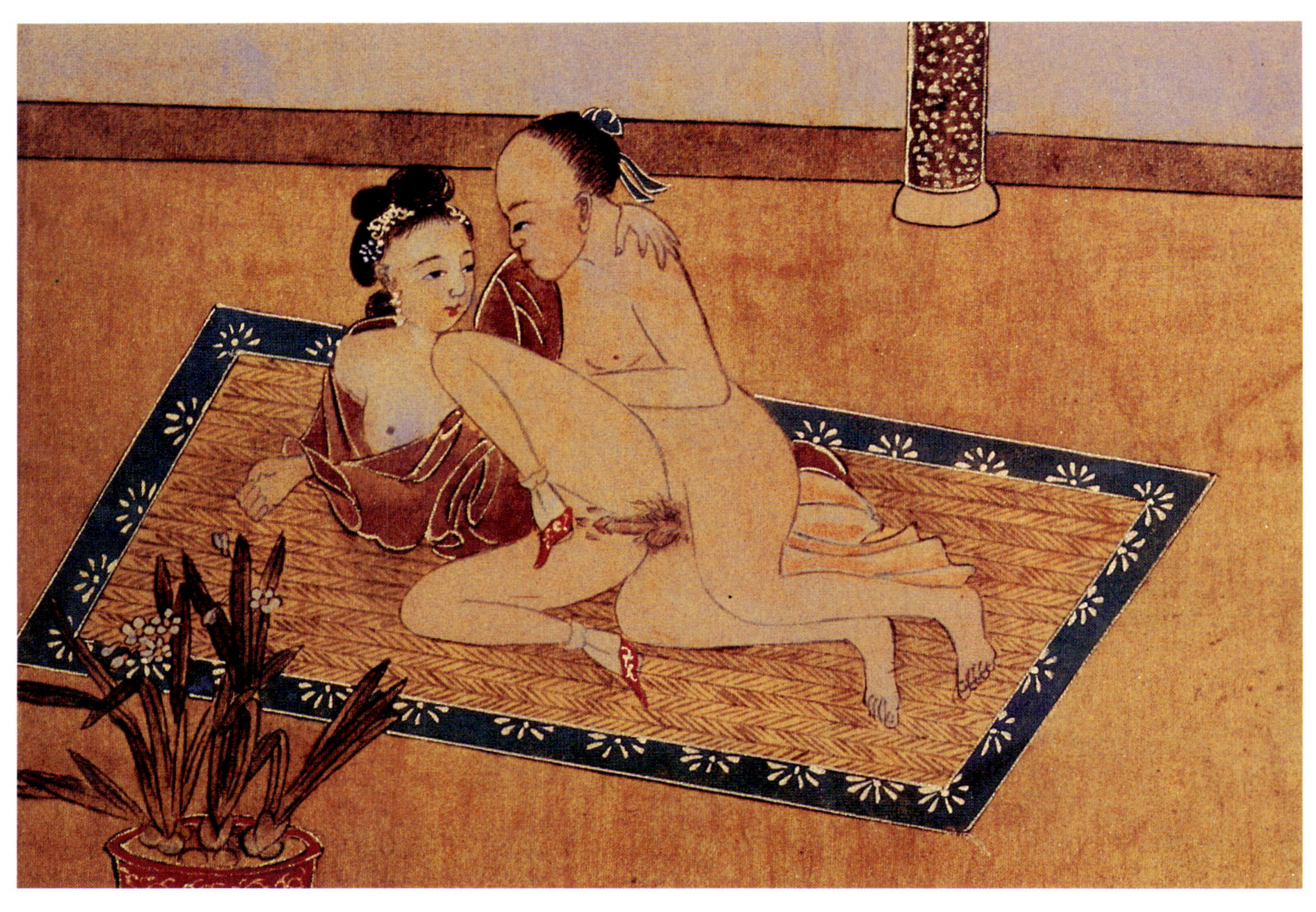

A Chinese couple make love upon a mat. The bowl of sprouting bulbs in the foreground symbolizes the upward flow of sexual energy produced by the correct practice of this therapeutic love posture.

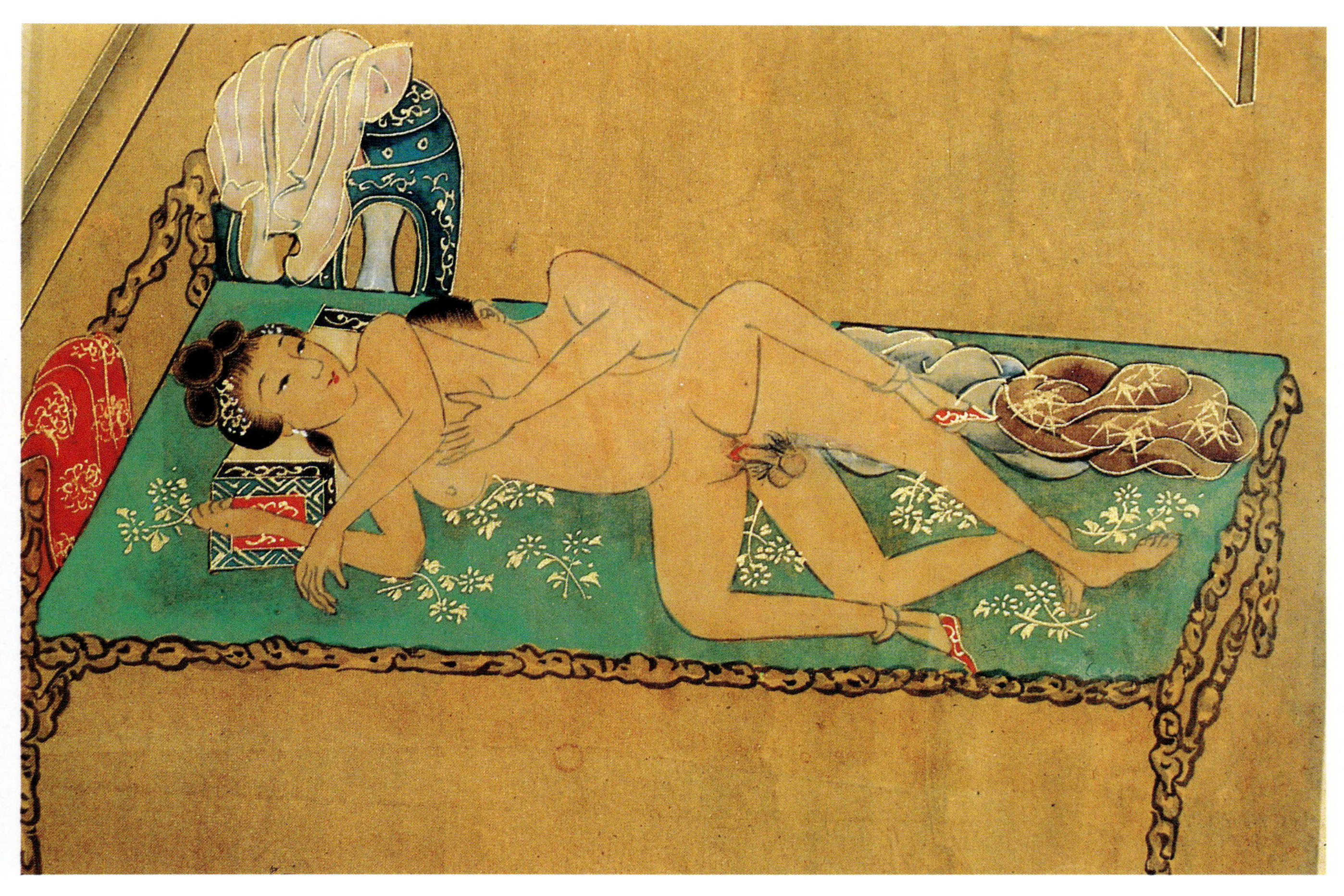

Here a Chinese couple, united in love upon an unusual ornate bamboo bed embellished with gold floral highlights, perform the Taoist love posture known as Mandarin Ducks.

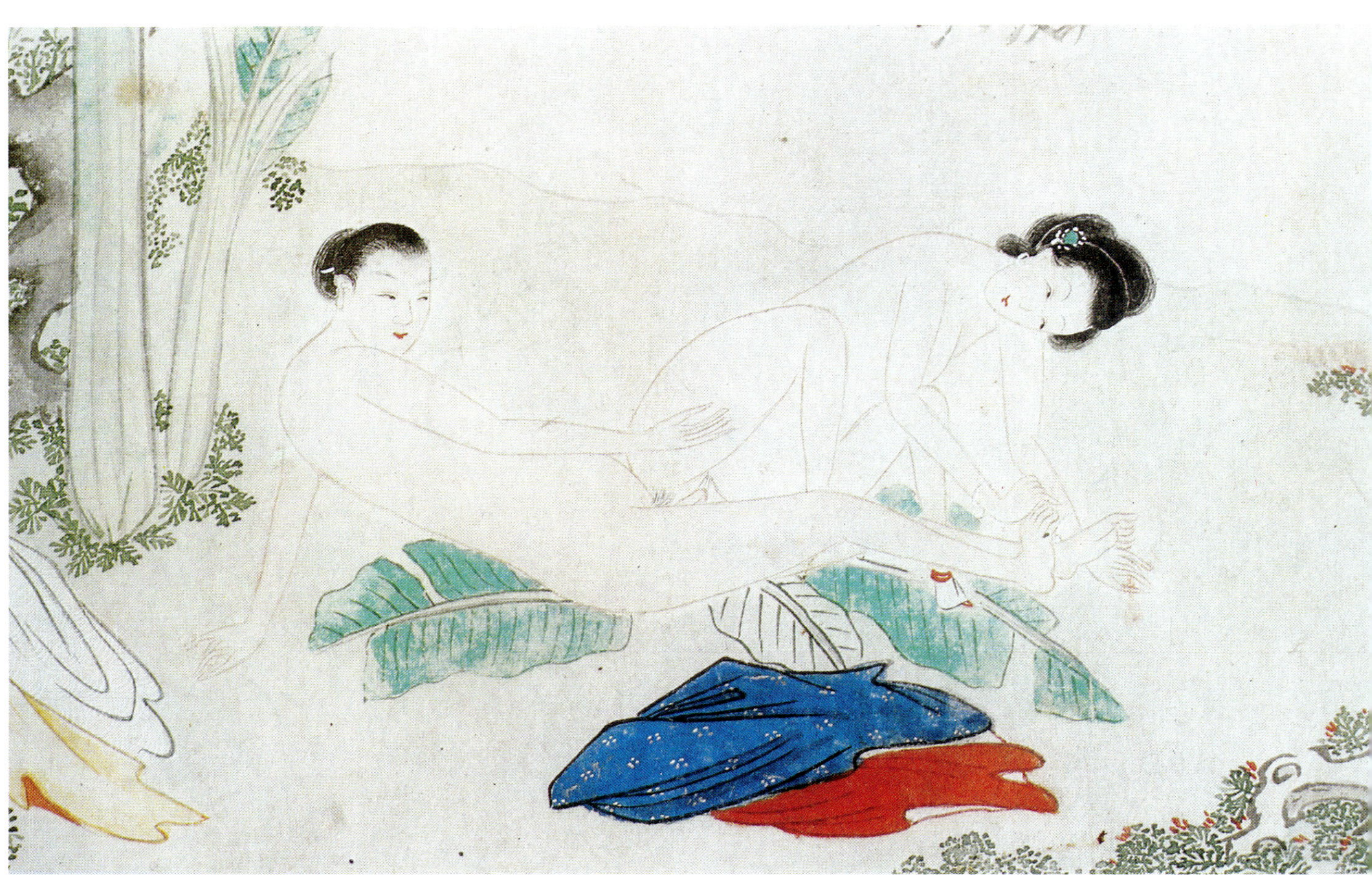

In a detail from a Chinese watercolor a couple are shown making love outdoors in the Taoist posture known as Overlapping Fish Scales. The lovers rest their naked bodies on banana leaves, their discarded clothes seeming like pools of color before them. The subtle palette of this composition accents the sensitivity expressed on the couple's faces.

Tiny drops of sweat are like a hundred fragrant pearls,
The sweet full breasts tremble;
The dew, like a gentle stream,
Reaches the Heart of the Peony.
They taste the joy of love in perfect harmony.
Chin P'ing Mei

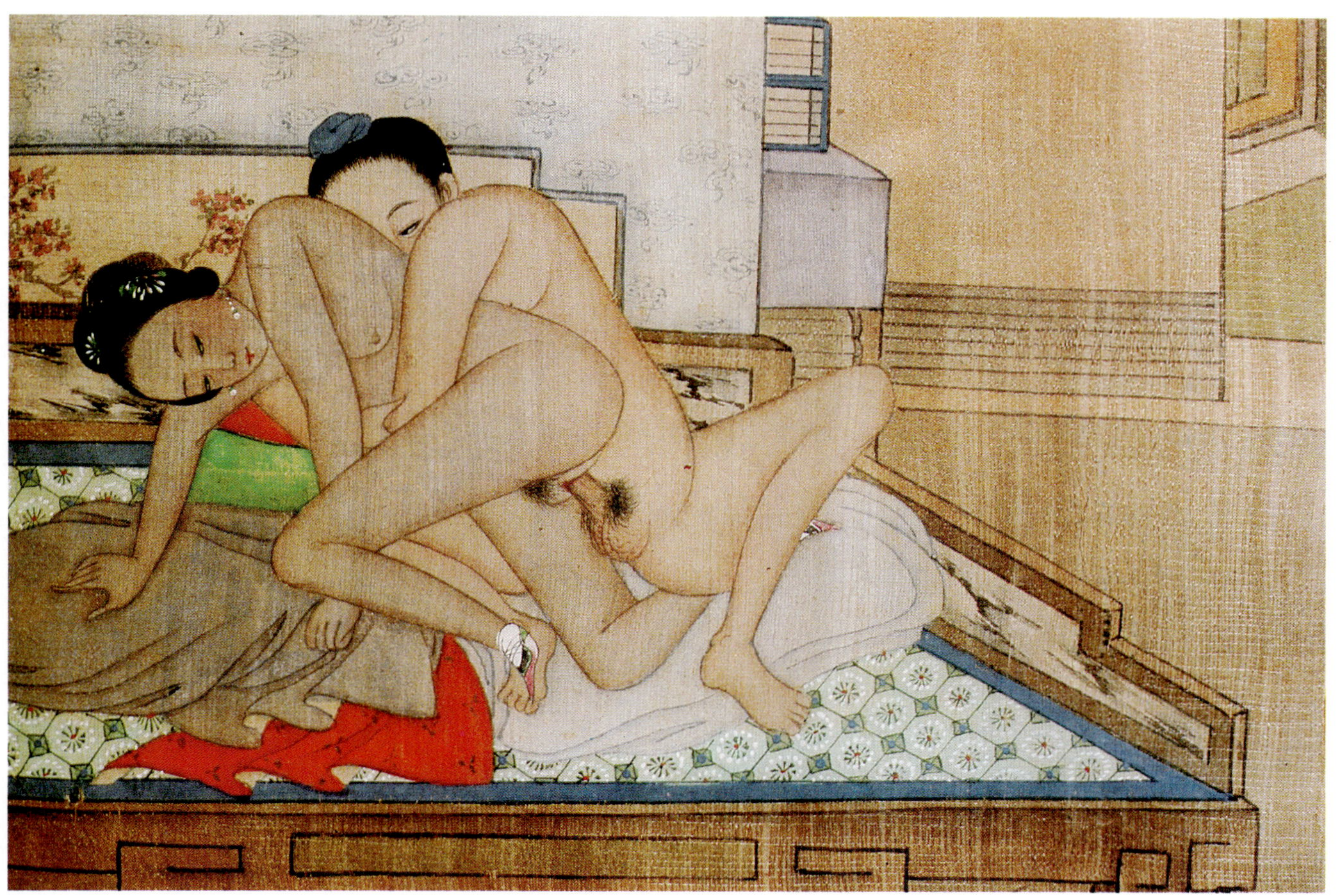

*In this detail of a larger painting the lovers perform the Taoist posture known as Jumping White Tiger.
The contrasting skin tones, angular composition, and fine details convey a sense of power and sensitivity.*

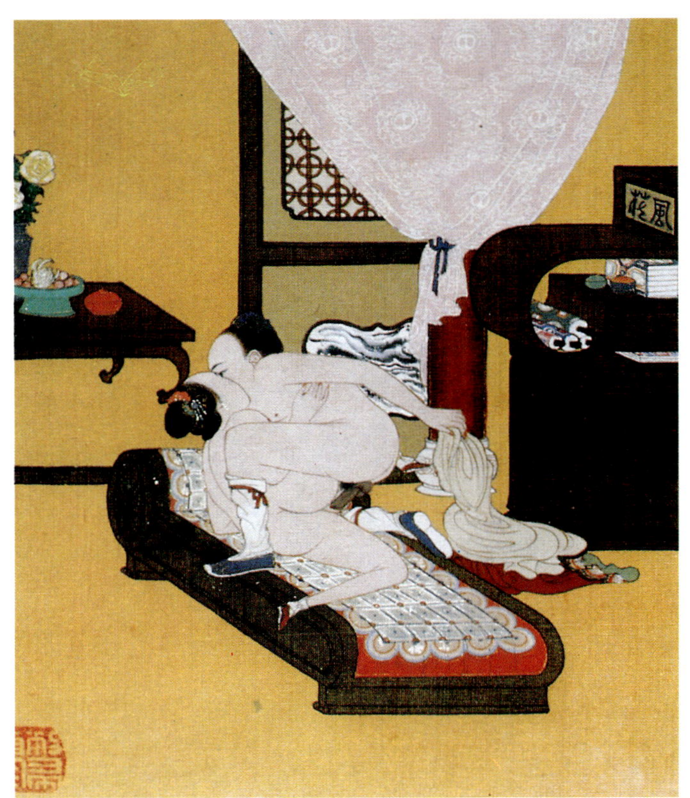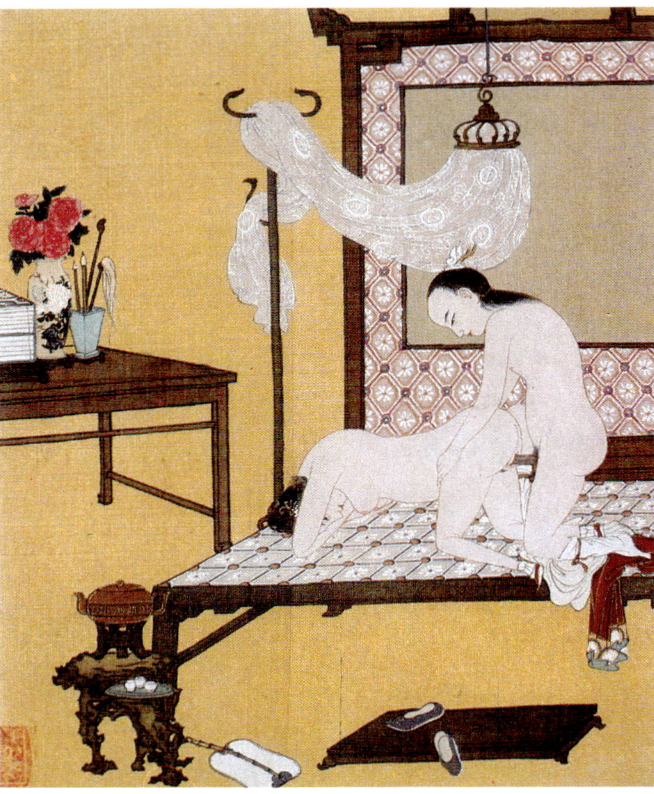

In this scene on the left, a Chinese couple are shown making love in a low bed, their movement caught as if frozen in time. As the man takes the active role, his partner turns on her side to complete a therapeutic love posture devised for the concentration of semen. On the right, a Chinese couple make love in the classical Taoist posture known as Tiger's Tread. The lovers support themselves upon a bed, which has a mosquito net placed over a nearby rack. Flowers, books, and paintbrushes stand on a nearby table.

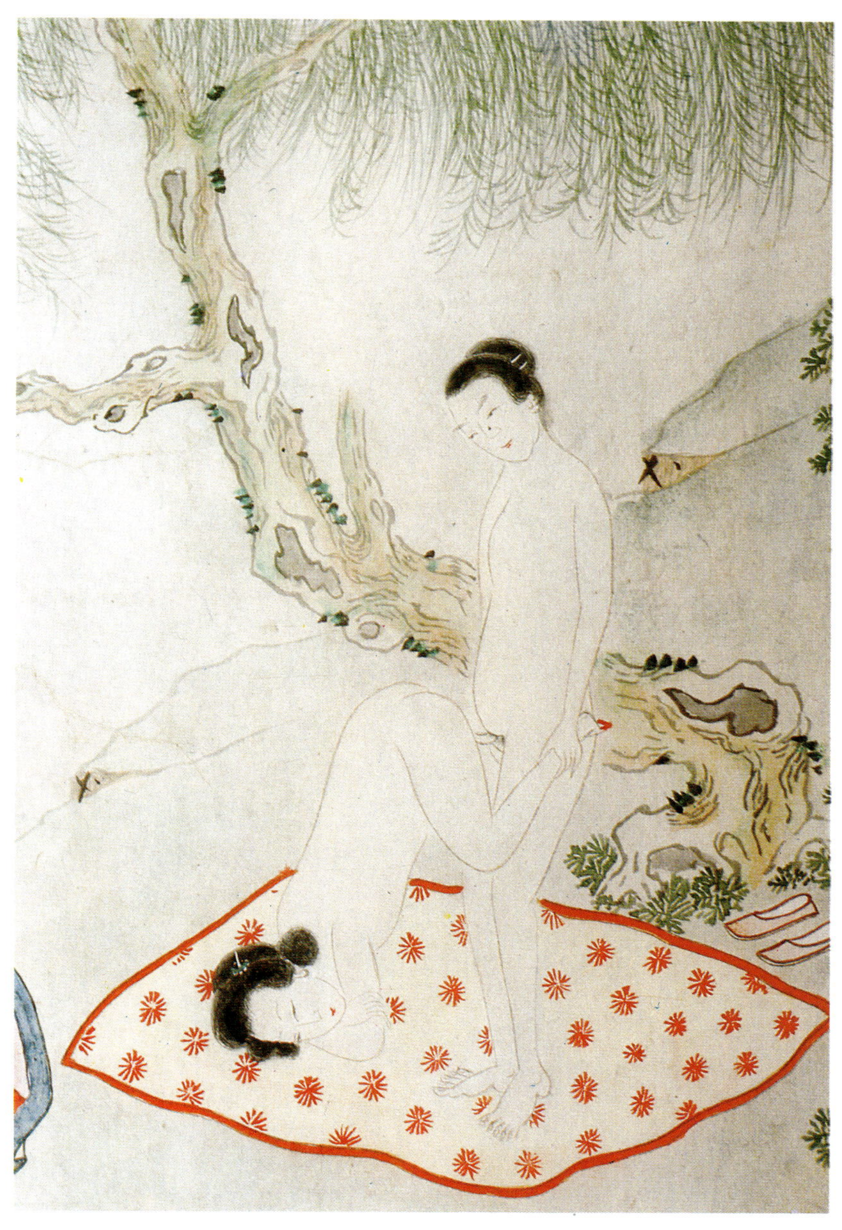

A Chinese couple make love on a cream and red mat beneath a willow tree. In this detail from a fine watercolor the lovers perform a variation of the Taoist posture known as *Donkeys in the Third Moon of Spring*. The old willow tree suggests constancy and longevity.

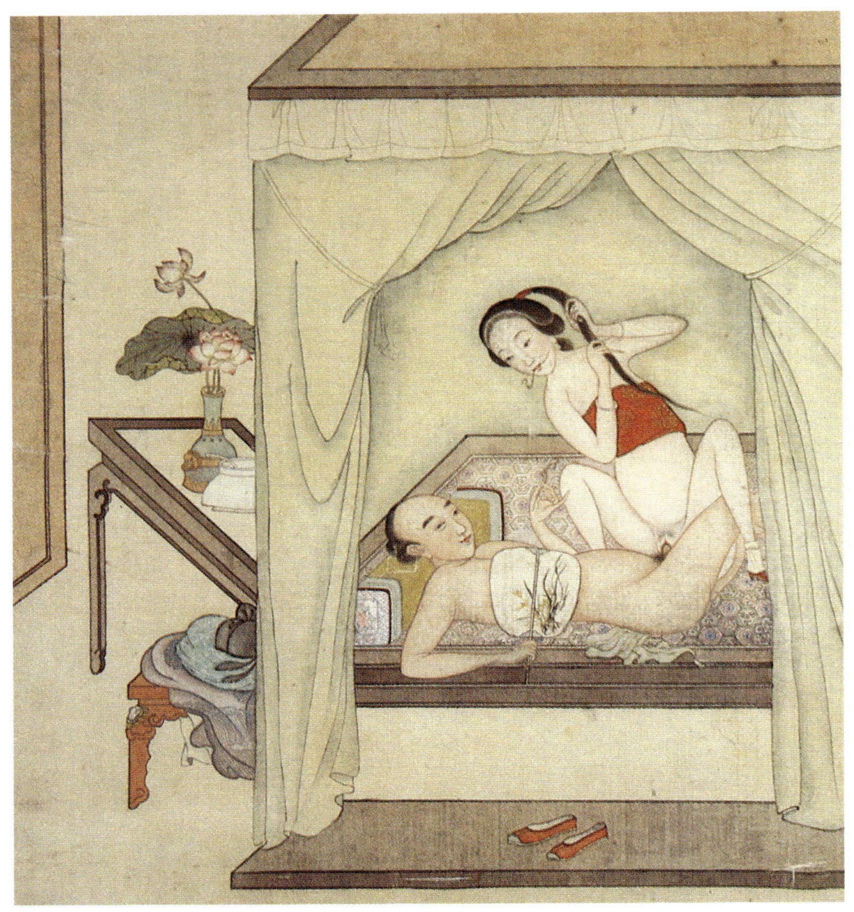

She made the bedstead ready, provided with the rarest luxuries,
including a bronze censer for scenting the quilts.
She let down the bed-curtains to the floor.
The mattresses and coverlets were piled up,
the pointed pillows lay across them.
Then she shed her upper robe and took off her undergarment,
revealing her white body, with thin bones and soft flesh.
When then we made love with each other
her body was soft and moist like ointment.

Mei-jen-fu of Szu-ma Hsiang-ju

A Chinese couple are shown in erotic union upon a canopied green-curtained bed. The man reclines and fans himself while his precious consort squats over him in the Taoist posture described by the Plain Girl in her Discourse on the Eight Benefits as "good for increasing the blood." Lotuses bloom in a vase to one side as the Initiatress of Love takes a moment to fix her hair.

Vermilion bed, exquisitely curtained;
Flower tapestry adorning the wall.
Scented oil lamp shining brightly;
Beautiful women fill the palace with love.
Ch'u Yuan

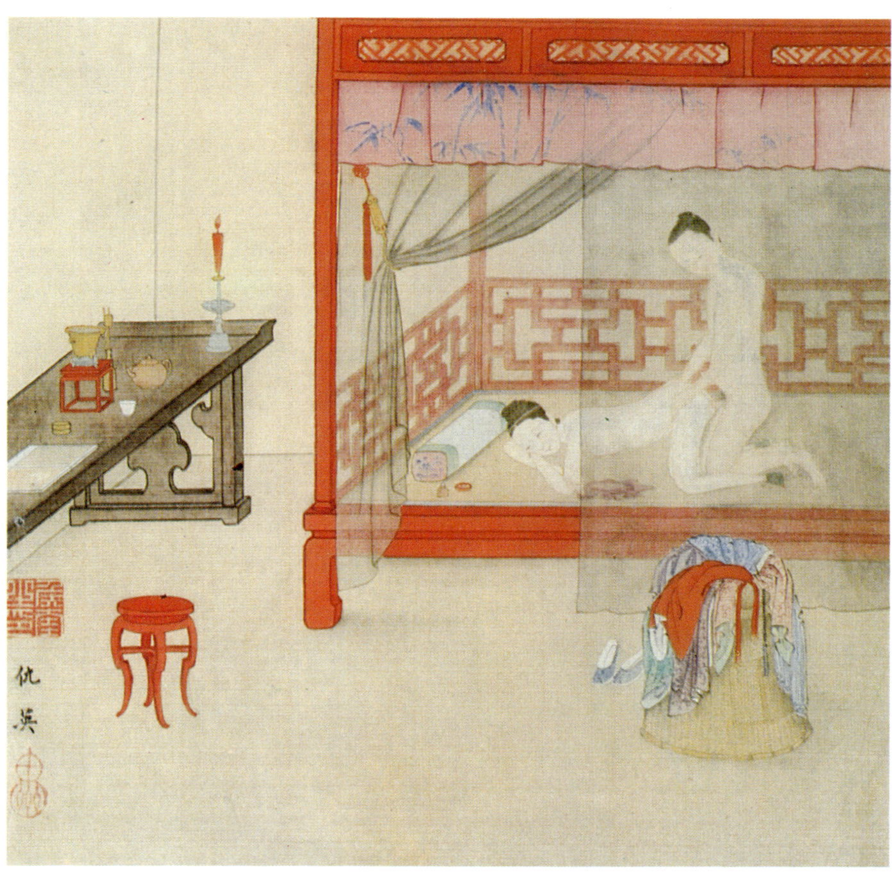

This exquisite scene shows a Chinese couple making love on a red lacquer canopied bed while a crimson candle burns nearby on a table. These lovers are performing the Taoist posture known as Jumping White Tiger, in which entry is made from the rear. Their pale bodies, glimpsed tantalizingly through diaphanous drapes, contrast with the vermilion color of the furnishings.

51

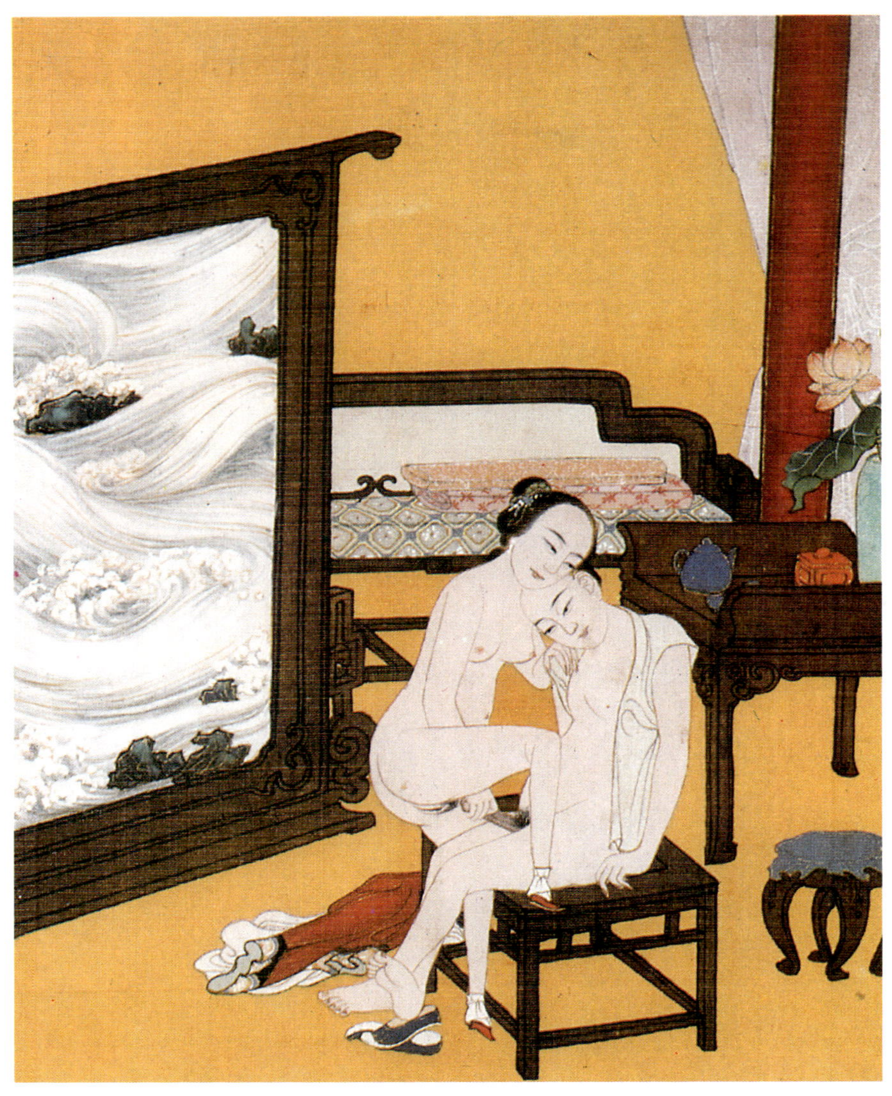

Chinese lovers are shown in dalliance before a beautifully painted screen of swirling waves, symbolic of torrents of passion. She takes his "Love Weapon" in her hand and brings it close to her "Pleasure Portal," to unite in a variation of the Taoist posture known as Shouting Monkey Embracing a Tree. The open lotus in a vase suggests the spiritual quality of their union.

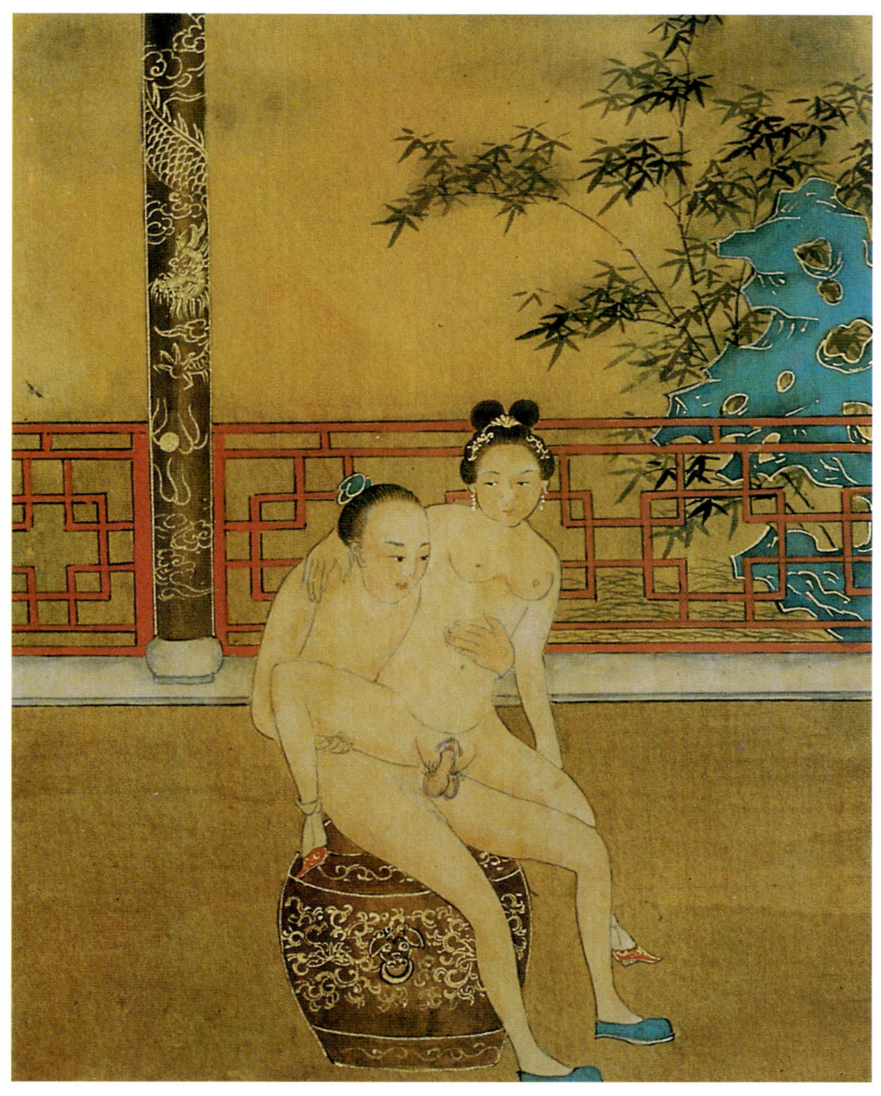

A Chinese couple are seated on an ornate stool placed on a veranda decorated with red railings and a dragon column. The woman is seated upon her partner in the Taoist posture known as Mountain Goat Facing a Tree. The unusual use of gold to create elaborate motifs is particularly pleasing in this fine composition.

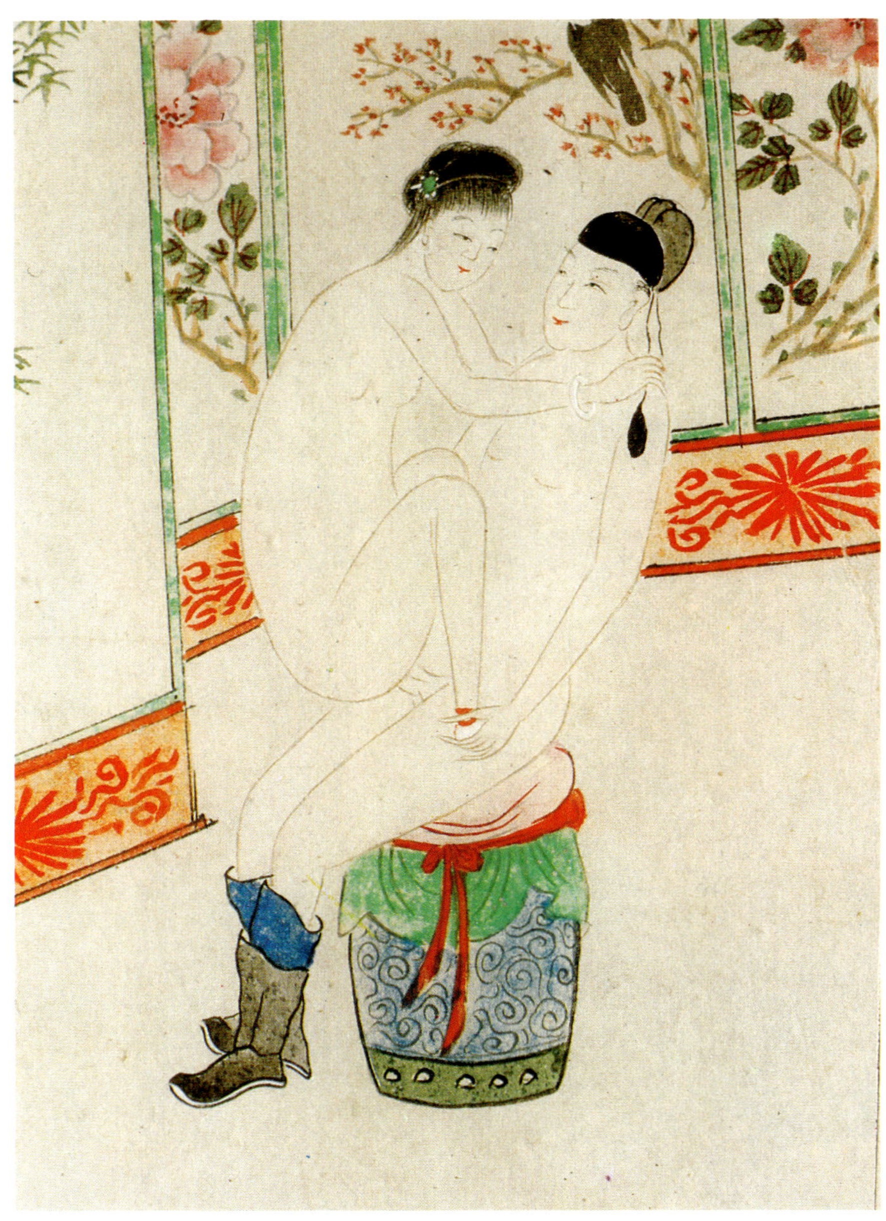

In this detail from a watercolor a Chinese couple are shown making love in a version of the Taoist posture known as Shouting Monkey Embracing a Tree. The man sits on a high stool sheltered by a screen exquisitely decorated with flowers and birds; his partner squats over him and gently lowers her "Love Cavern" over his "Warrior" while embracing him around the neck.

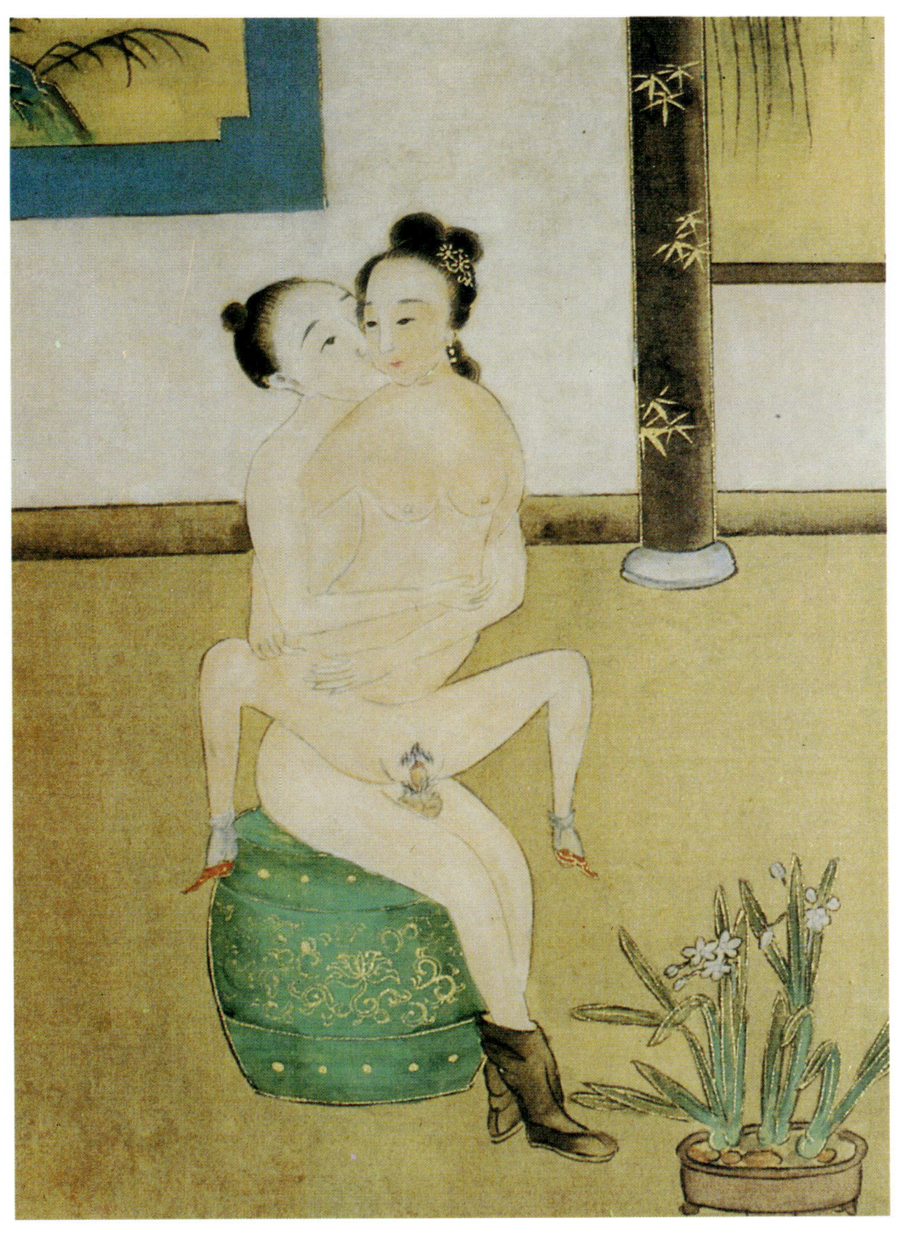

A Chinese couple make love within the confines of their house. The man embraces his partner around the waist as she squats upon his erect "Love Weapon." Their love posture is known as Mountain Goat Facing a Tree; the rejuvenative potential of this type of Taoist position is suggested by the bowl of sprouting bulbs in the foreground.

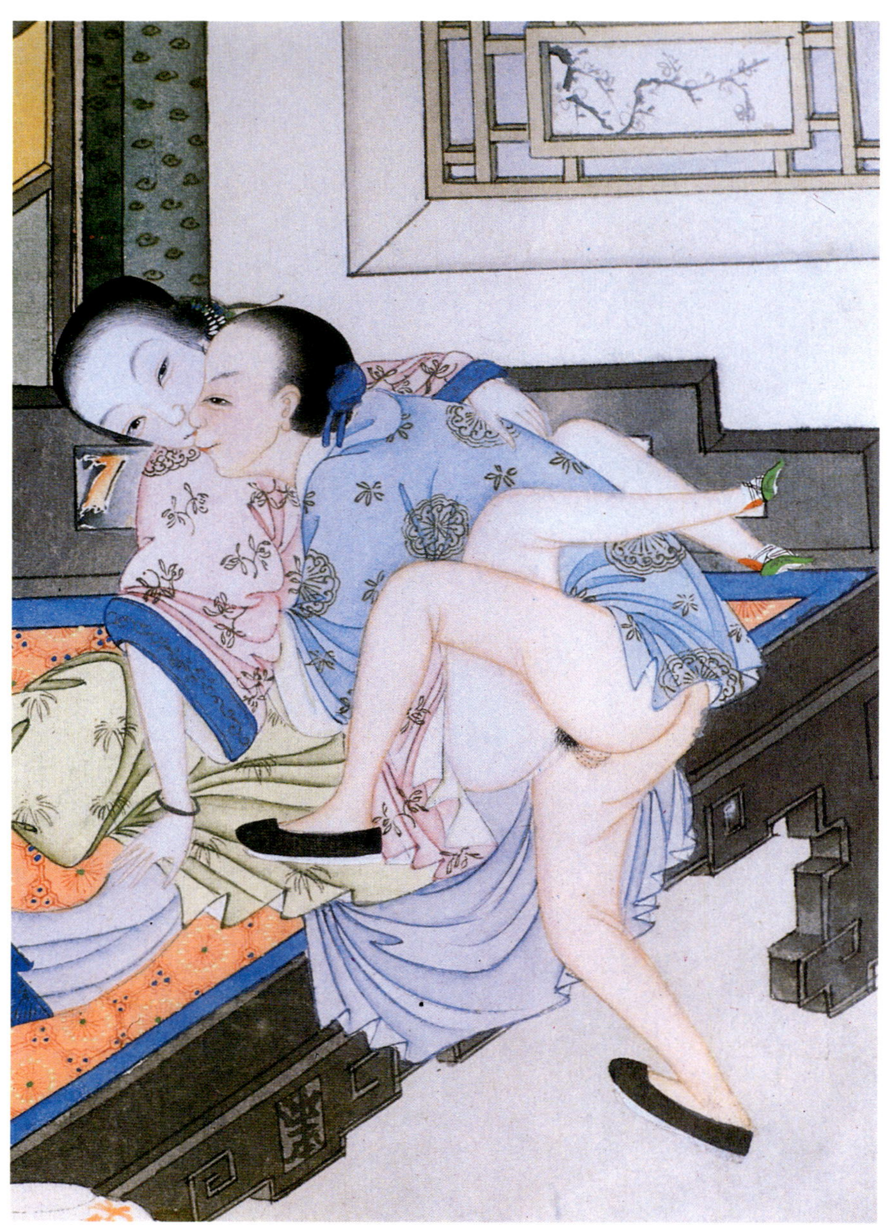

In this detail from a fine Chinese watercolor a richly dressed couple are shown making love in the classical posture known as Soaring Seagulls. The man approaches the bed as his partner wraps her legs tightly around his waist; drawing her to him, he inserts his "Jade Stalk" within her "Precious Gate." The delicate palette, tender expressions, and fine details make this a particularly sensitive study in eroticism.

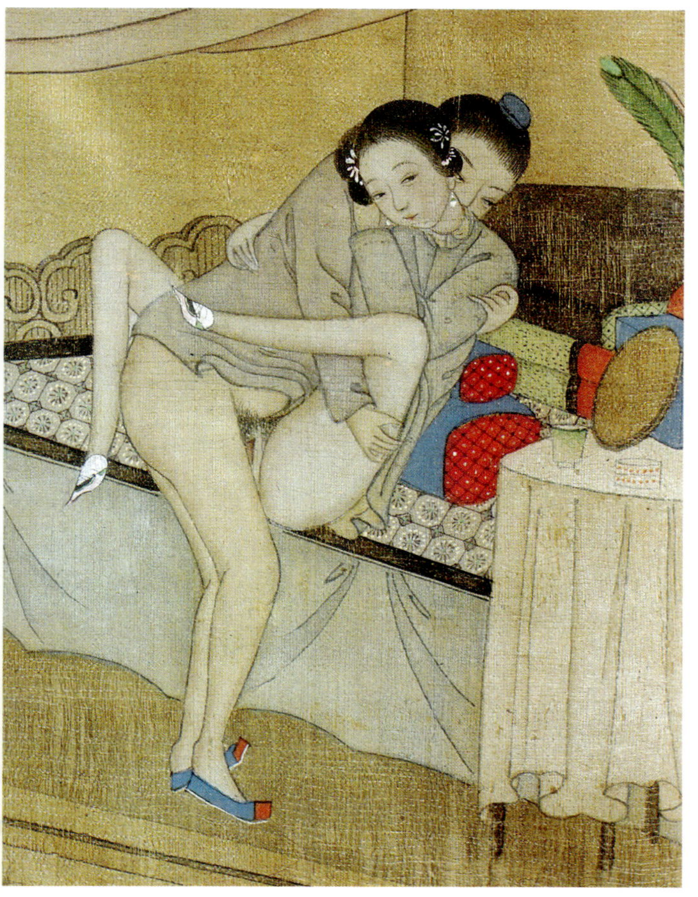 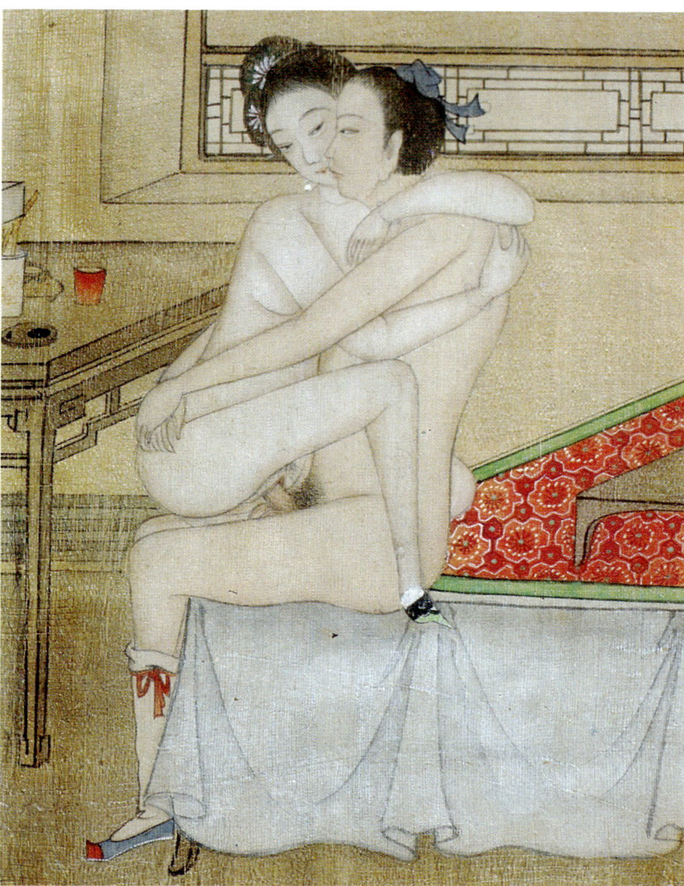

On the left, a partly clothed Chinese couple make love in the *Soaring Seagulls* posture. *The man stands and unites with his partner, who supports herself on crimson and blue pillows. In the scene on the right, a couple make love in the classical posture known as Shouting Monkey Embracing a Tree. The man sits upright and unites his "Jade Flute" with her "Anemone of Love."*

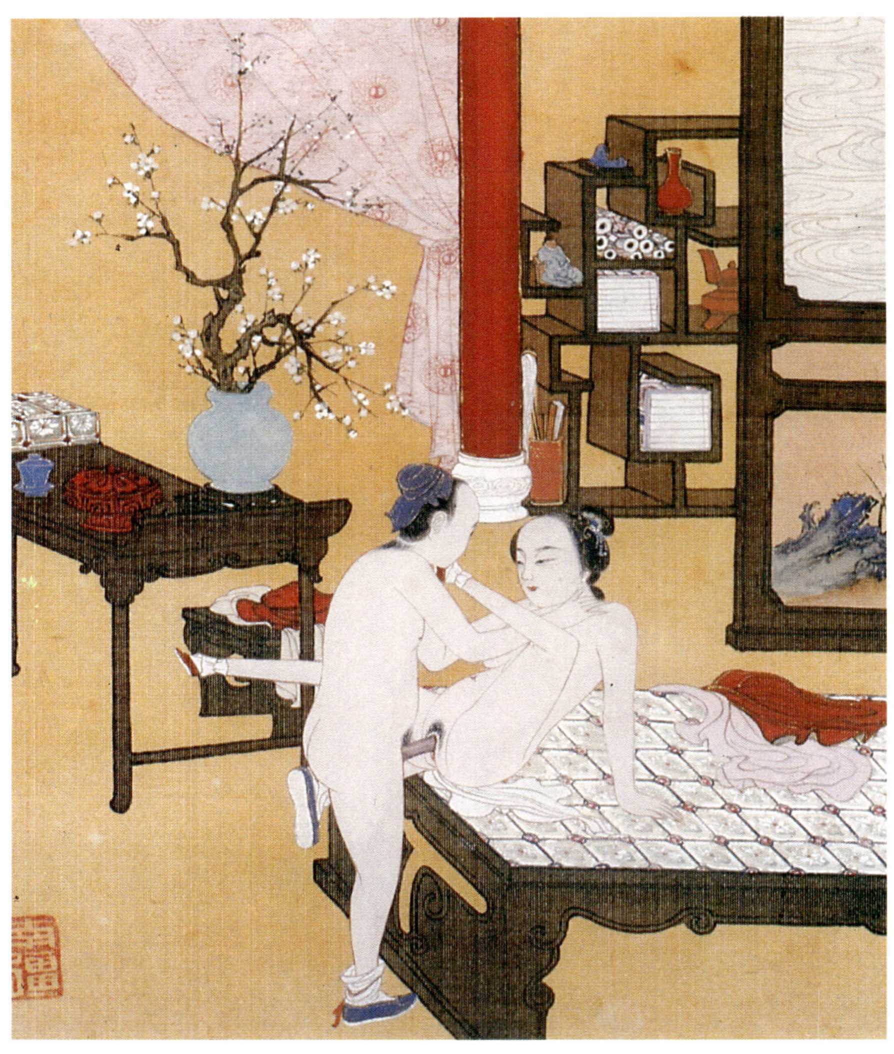

In another variation of the Taoist posture known as Soaring Seagulls a Chinese couple make love using a bed for support. Albums and scrolls fill the shelves next to a crimson column draped by a pink curtain. On a nearby table a vase of bursting blossoms suggests renewal and sudden awakening through the power of passion.

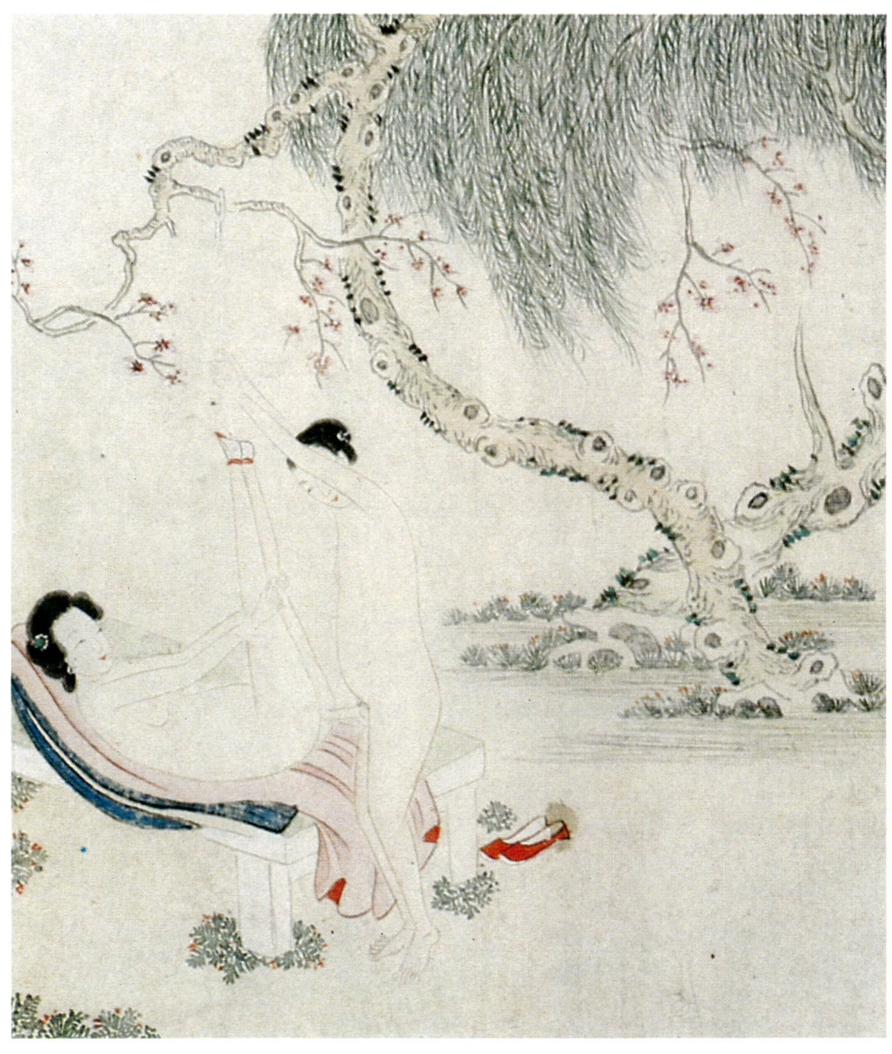

A Chinese couple make love in an outdoor setting. The woman leans backward on a bench, her feet raised high and suspended from the branches of a tree by silken cords. The man's "Jade Scepter" enters his partner's "Pleasure House" as he stands before her. This amusing scene delightfully illustrates the joys of spontaneous innovation in the "Battle of Love."

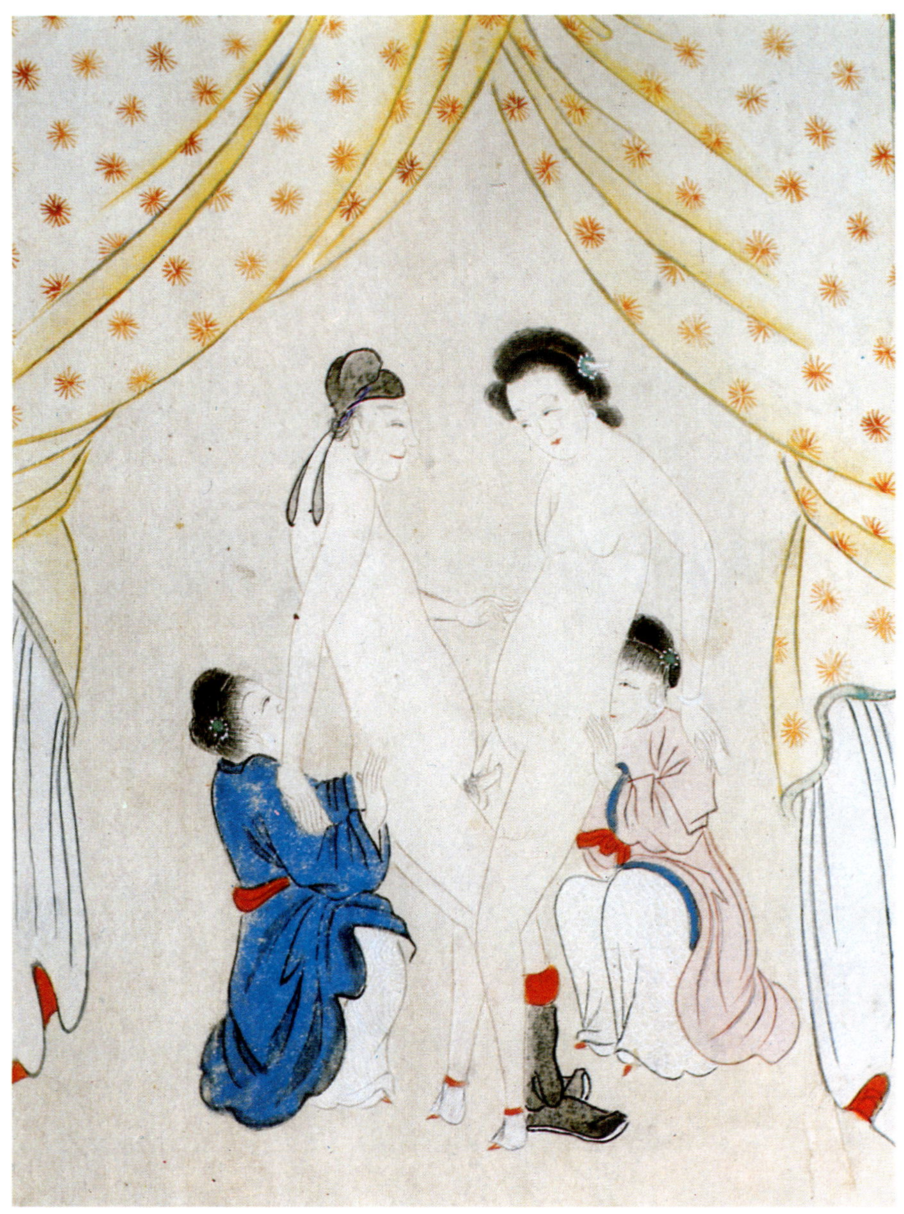

Here an extraordinary love rite is revealed. A naked Chinese noble couple stand and make love in the classical Taoist posture known as Bamboo near the Altar; their bodies are supported by two servants, who aid in their movements of love. The stark whiteness of the naked bodies contrasts with the pink and blue robes of the servants; a yellow floral canopy is carefully draped into sensual shapes, adding to the mood of eroticism.

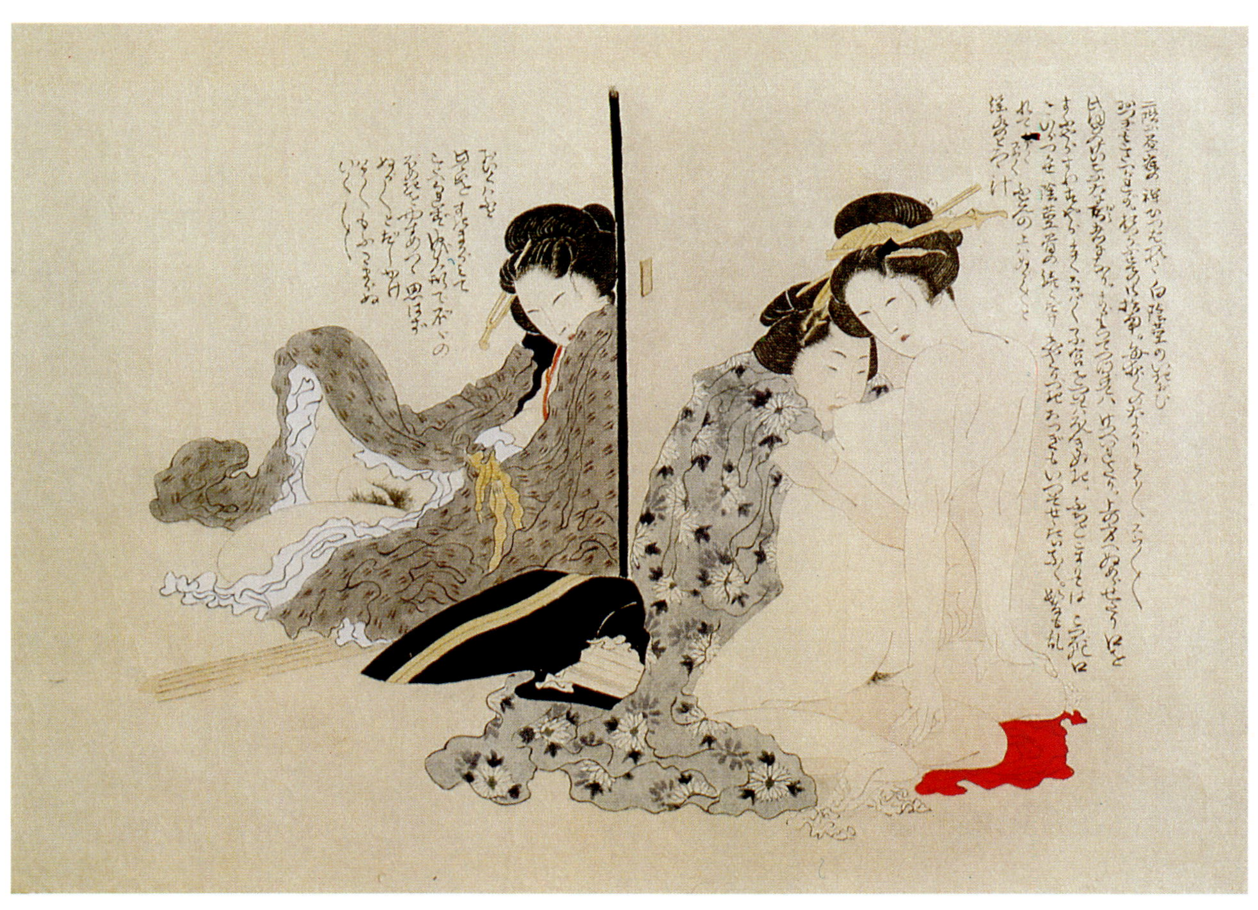

This *Shunga* painting shows two distinct erotic scenes. To the right side of a screen a Japanese couple unite together in a seated love posture, the woman arching her naked white body toward her partner as he caresses her left breast. To the left of the screen a solitary woman fondles her "Jade Gateway."

It is ten times more pleasant to make love during
the day than at night. The particular attraction
lies in being able to behold the other's nakedness,
for such a sight increases the desire.

Jou Pu Tuan

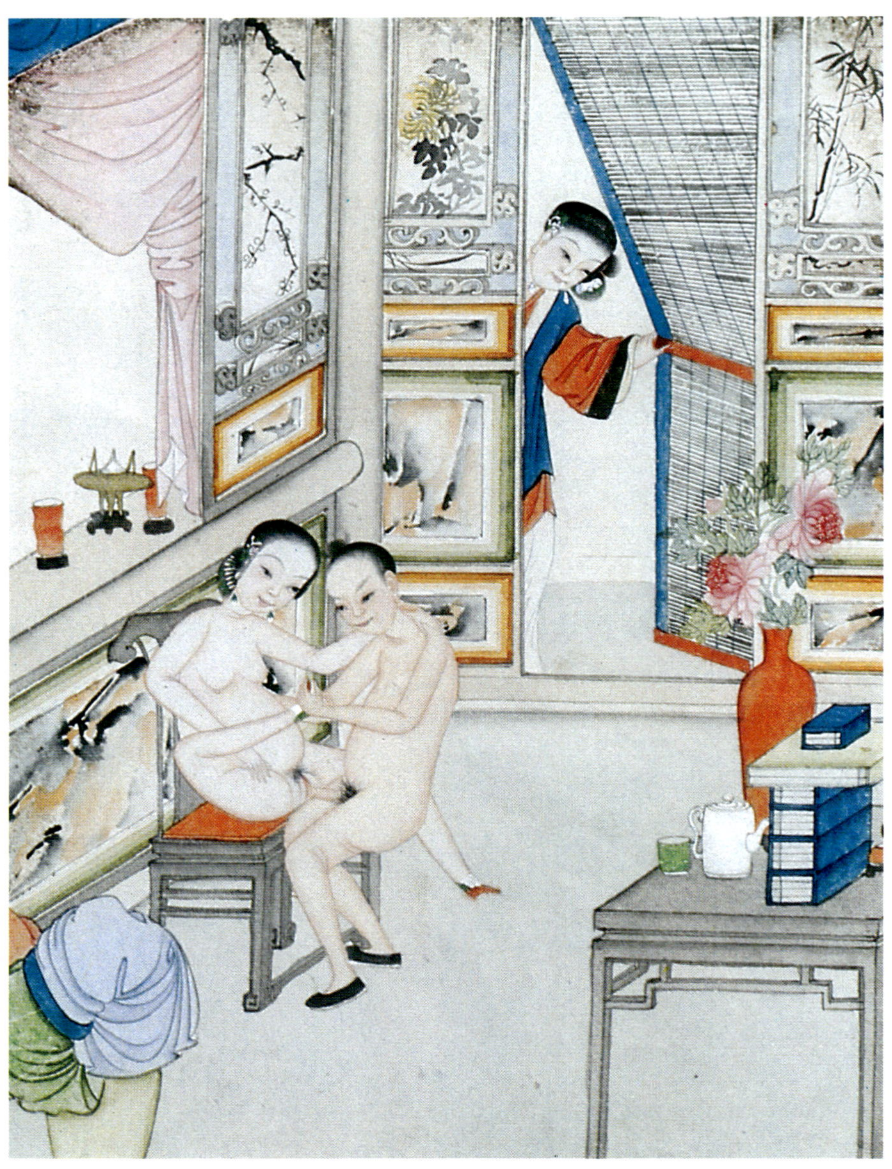

This fine watercolor depicts a Chinese couple making love within an elaborately decorated room. As the woman sits on a chair, her partner stands before her and unites his "Jade Stalk" with her "Precious Peony"; a second woman peers into the room.

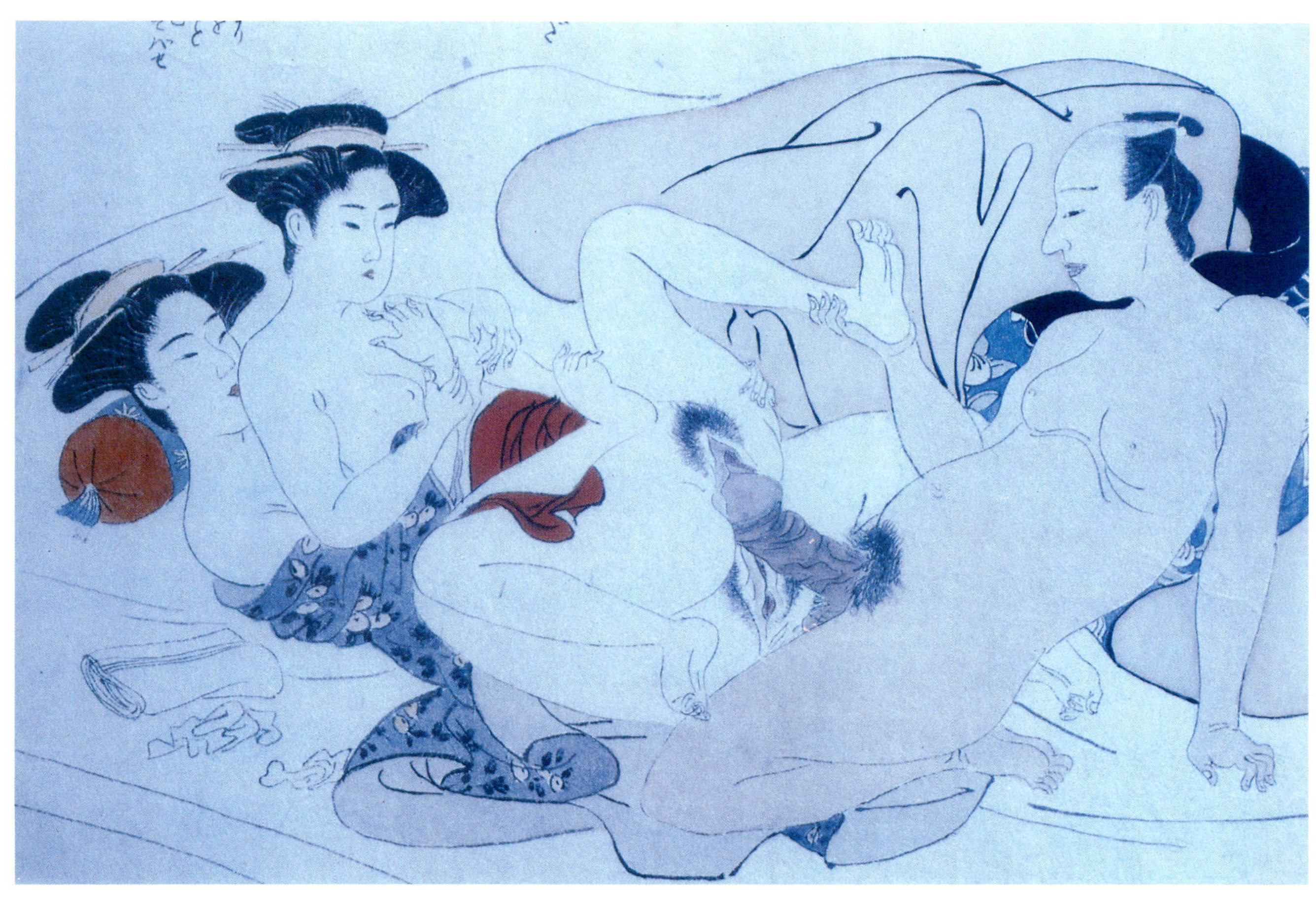

In this rare Shunga painting a Japanese man and two women make love in a version of the posture known as Two Dancing Female Phoenix Birds. The focus of the composition is the greatly enlarged "Faithful Servant" as it enters the "Precious Conch Shell" of the uppermost woman.

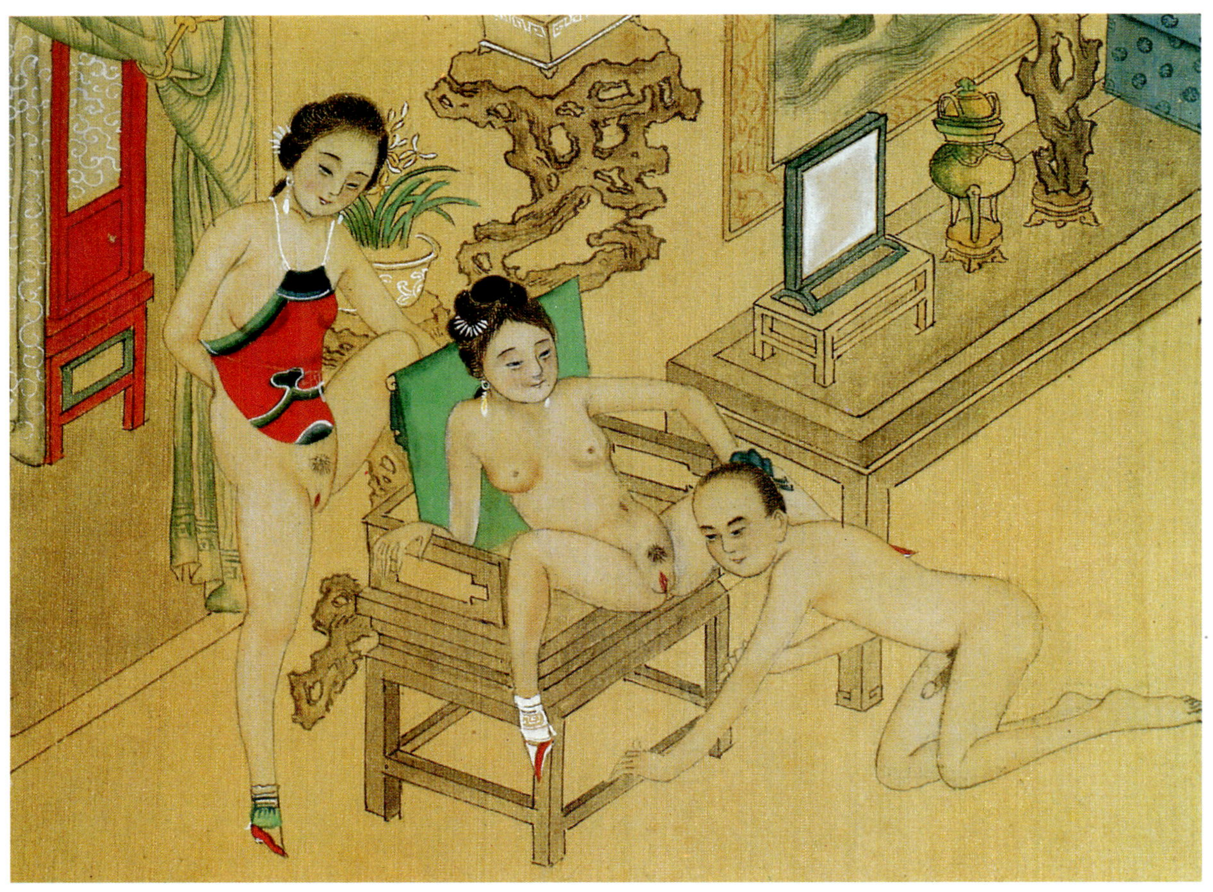

Here an interior scene is shown involving a single Chinese man with two women. The man kneels and approaches the exposed "Mysterious Gateway" of a woman who sits on a chair while a second woman, wearing only a small crimson apron, stands in attendance.

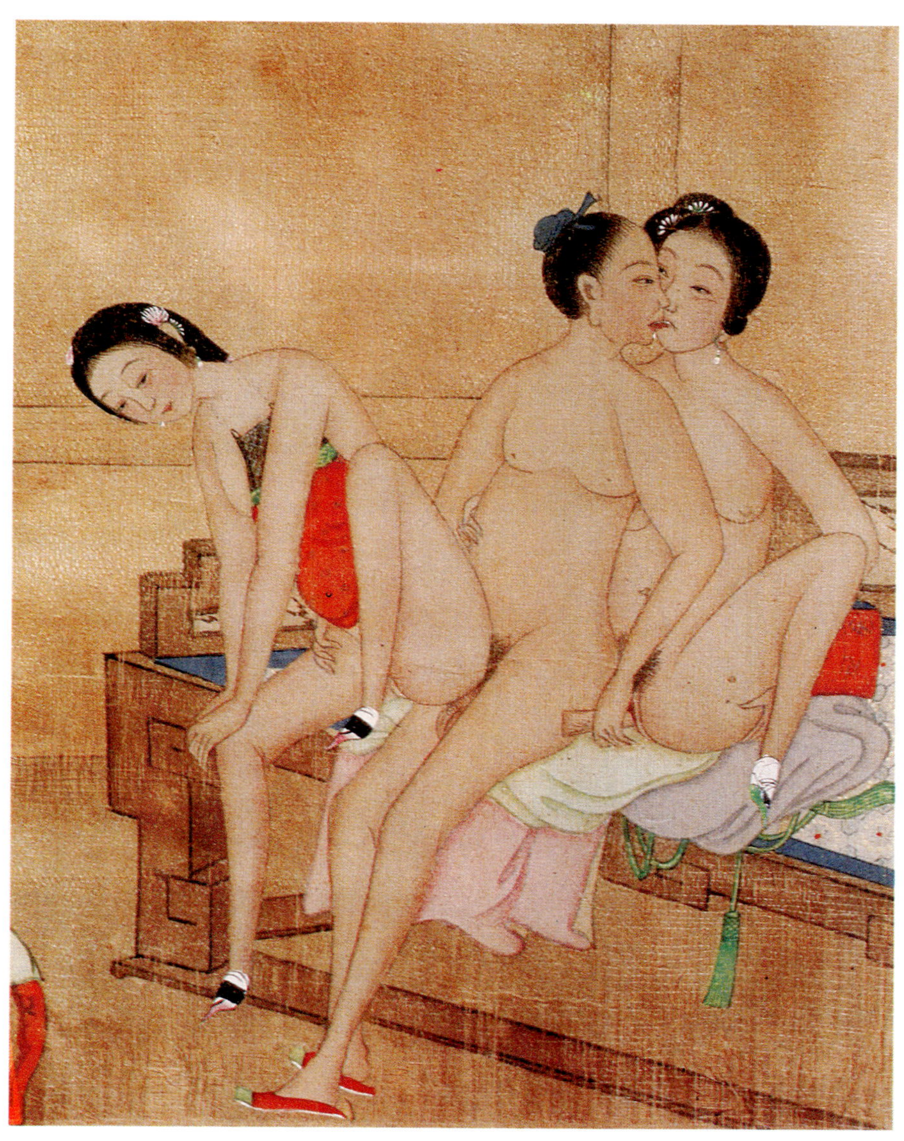

In this detail a Chinese man makes love with two women simultaneously, while seated upon a wooden bed. As he unites with one woman in the Taoist posture known as Mountain Goat Facing a Tree, the man uses a sexual aid to satisfy the second woman, whom he is also kissing. In Chinese polygamous society, techniques were developed to enable a man to satisfy each wife or concubine while circulating the sexual energy among all participants.

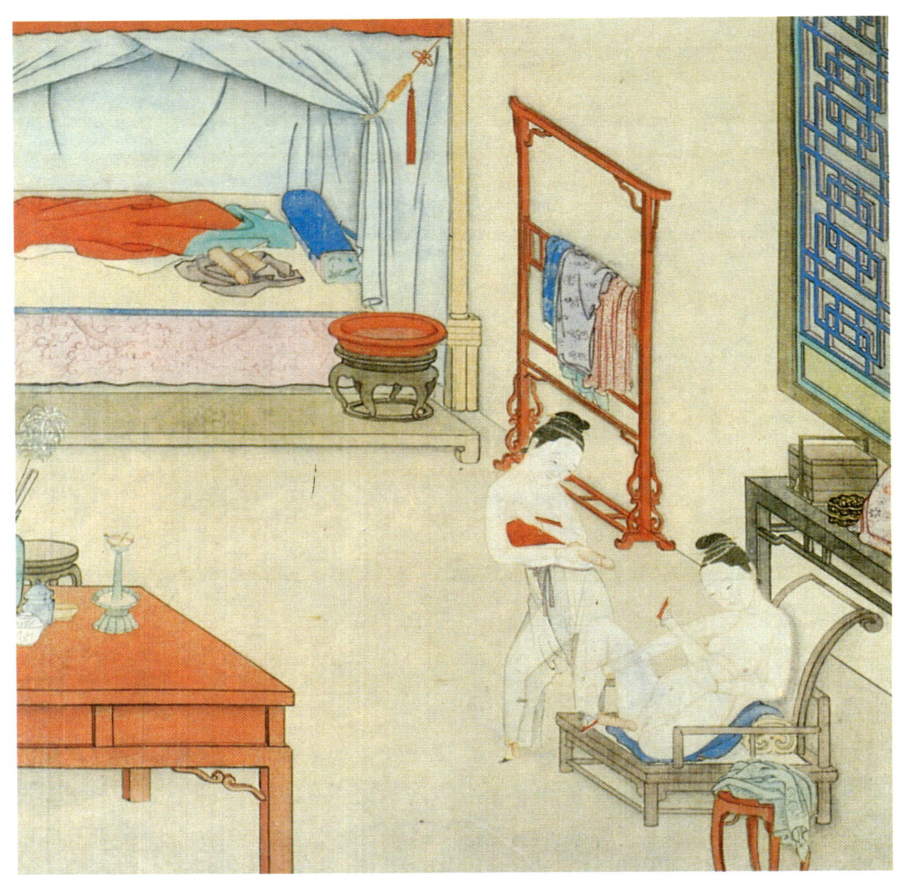

Two Chinese women are shown in a moment of intimacy. One sits naked in a low chair, a substitute phallus attached to her heel for self-gratification, while the other woman stands nearby, holding a second one. In Chinese culture such sexual aids were often employed in a harem setting.

Sometimes each Peony in turn
Slept with him until dawn.
Sometimes both shared him
Until midnight;
Finally, all loved each other
As the three came together as one.
Chao Hen

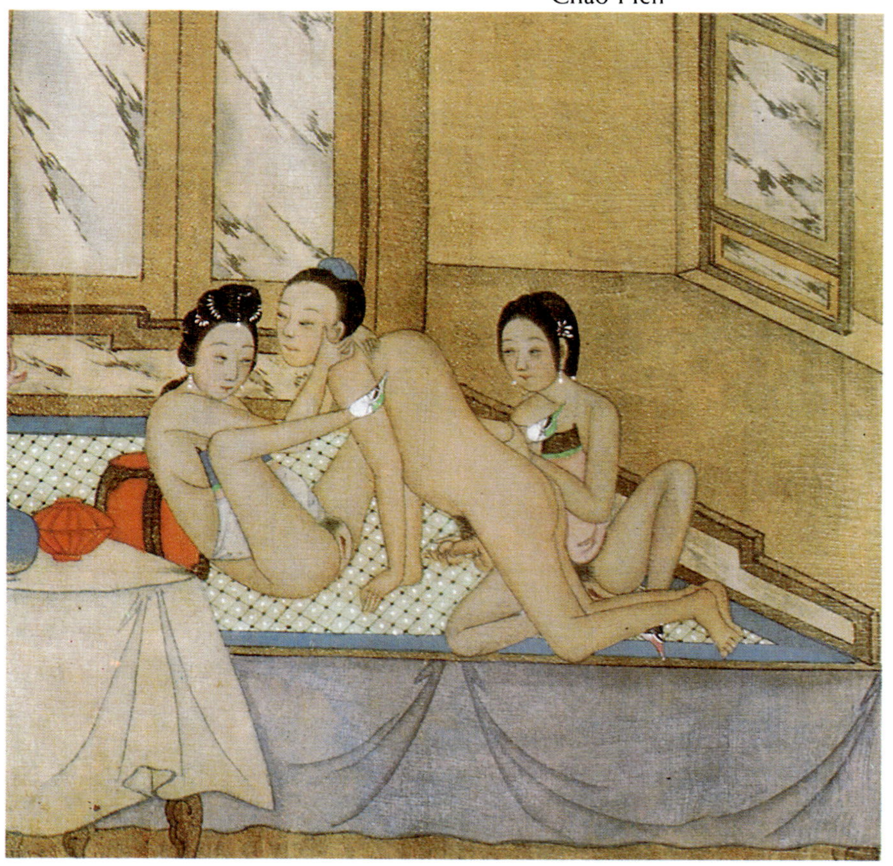

A Chinese man kneels on a bed and prepares to make love to two women, one of whom caresses his "Jade Stalk" while the other leans back with thighs apart and arms around his neck. It seems they are preparing for the Taoist posture known as Jungle Fowl. The muted colors and delicate treatment of facial expressions helps convey a mood of sensitive eroticism.

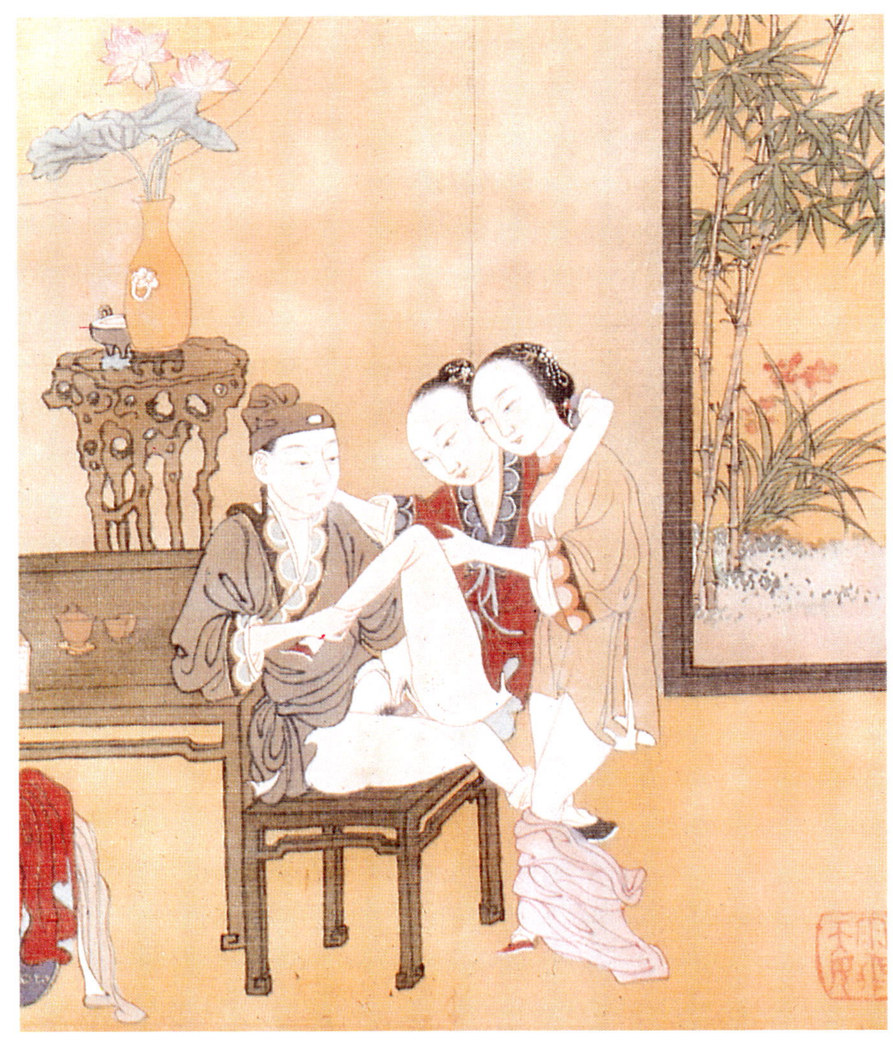

A partially dressed Chinese man is seated on a chair within an exquisitely decorated room. One woman lowers her "Cinnabar Crevice" over the man's "Positive Peak," assisted by a second partly clothed standing woman. This scene probably depicts a nobleman with two of his wives; the two blooming lotuses visible in a vase behind subtly suggest the satisfaction of both.

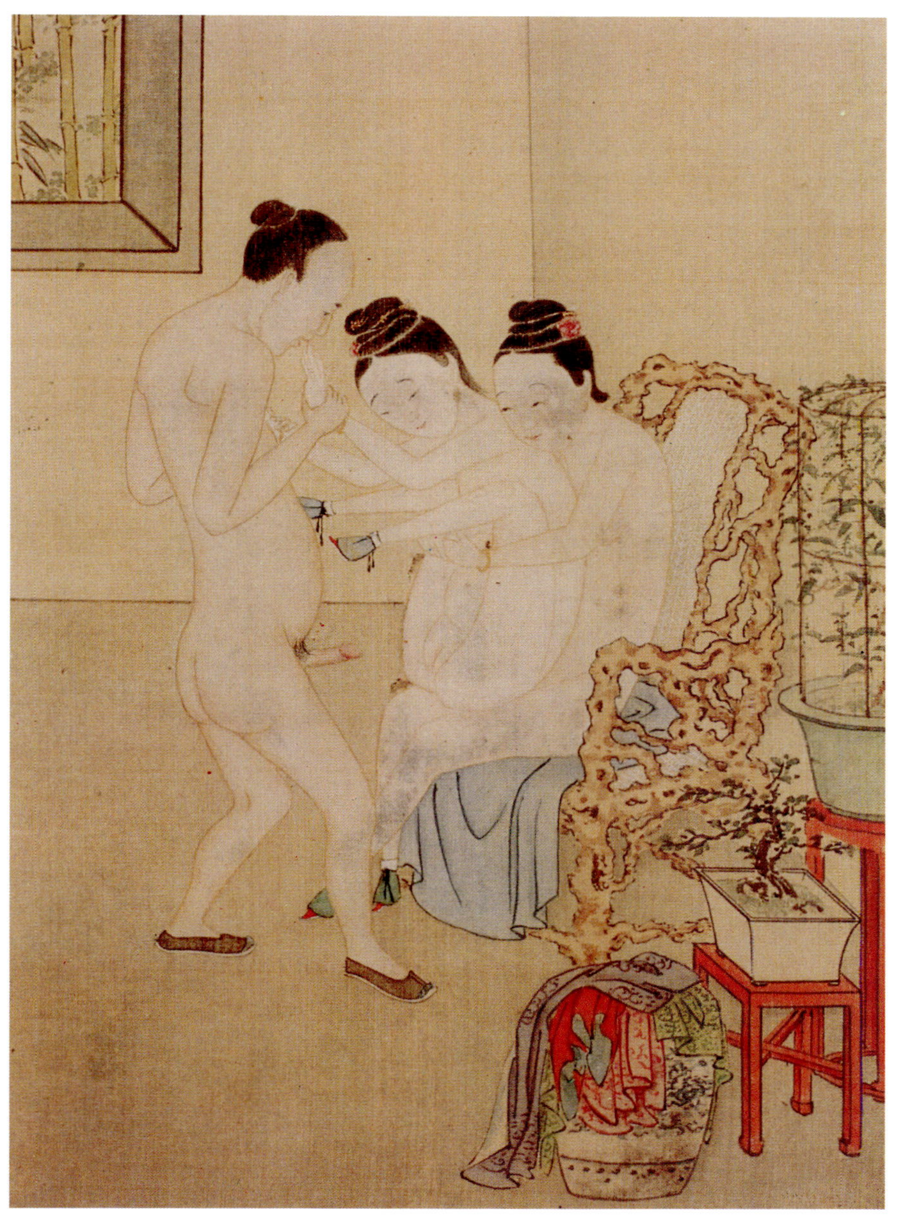

In this detail from a larger painting two naked Chinese women are shown seated on an ornate chair, one holding the other so as to allow penetration of the "Purple Peony" by the "Yang Pagoda" of the standing naked man. This scene may represent a husband with two wives or perhaps the sexual initiation of a young courtesan. The bonzai tree in the foreground symbolizes longevity, here realized through the successful harmonization of the Yin force of femininity.

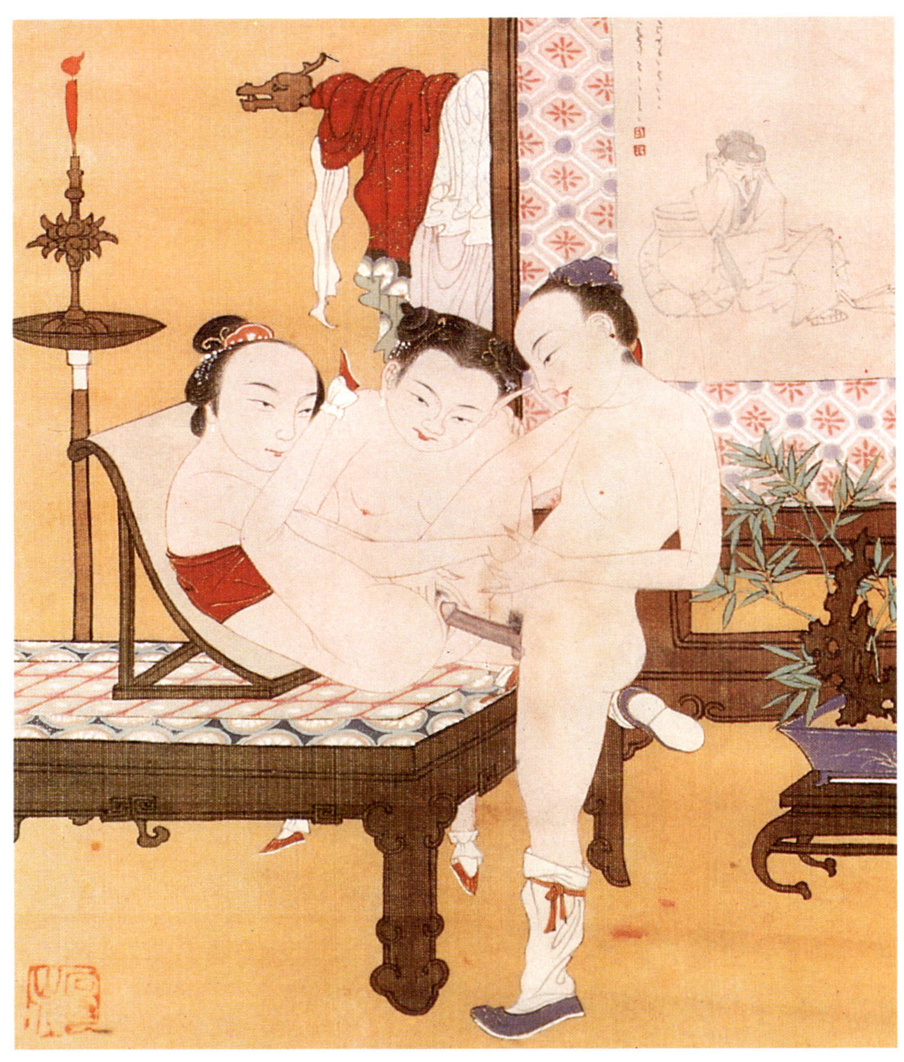

A Chinese man stands before a couch and inserts his "Positive Peak" into the "Honey Pot" of a woman supporting herself against a special back rest; a second woman assists as a crimson candle burns brightly to one side. The pot of bursting bamboo shoots, dragon-motif hanger, and portrait of a Taoist sage on the screen behind all suggest that this "secret dalliance" is an ancient rite for longevity.

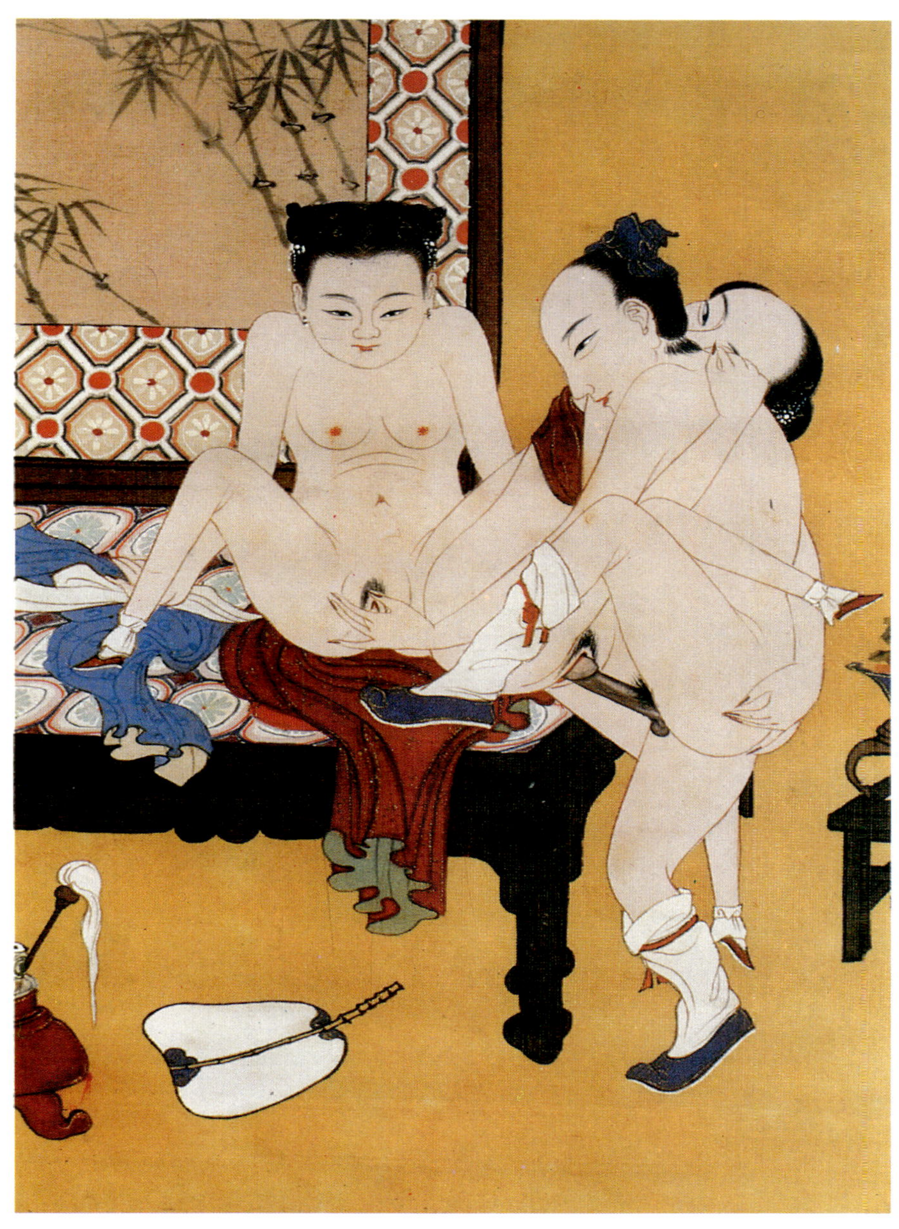

A Chinese man stands before a couch and gently enters the "Secret Cavern" of one woman with his "Crimson Bird" while probing the "Pleasure Portal" of a second woman, who exposes herself to him. Despite the plurality of this union, no trace of jealously can be seen on the faces of the women. The color composition of this painting is particularly effective in conveying the mood of intimacy.

There is a Secret Dalliance known as the Heavenly and Earthly Net whereby
people indulge in sexual play like the birds and beasts, many females with a
single male.

Tao An

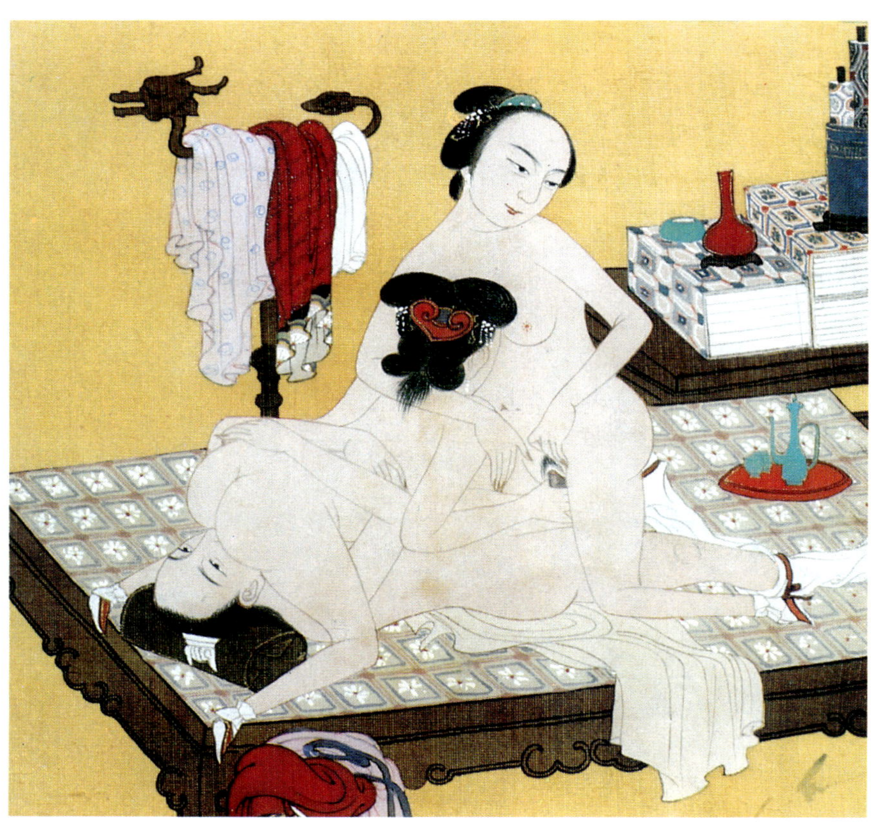

A Chinese man reclines upon a couch and unites with one woman in a therapeutic love posture for "increasing the blood" while practicing oral love with a second woman, who sits over him and caresses his "Jade Scepter" as it moves within the "Anemone of Love." A pyramid of forces is created by the conjoined bodies. Pillow books are piled high on a nearby table.

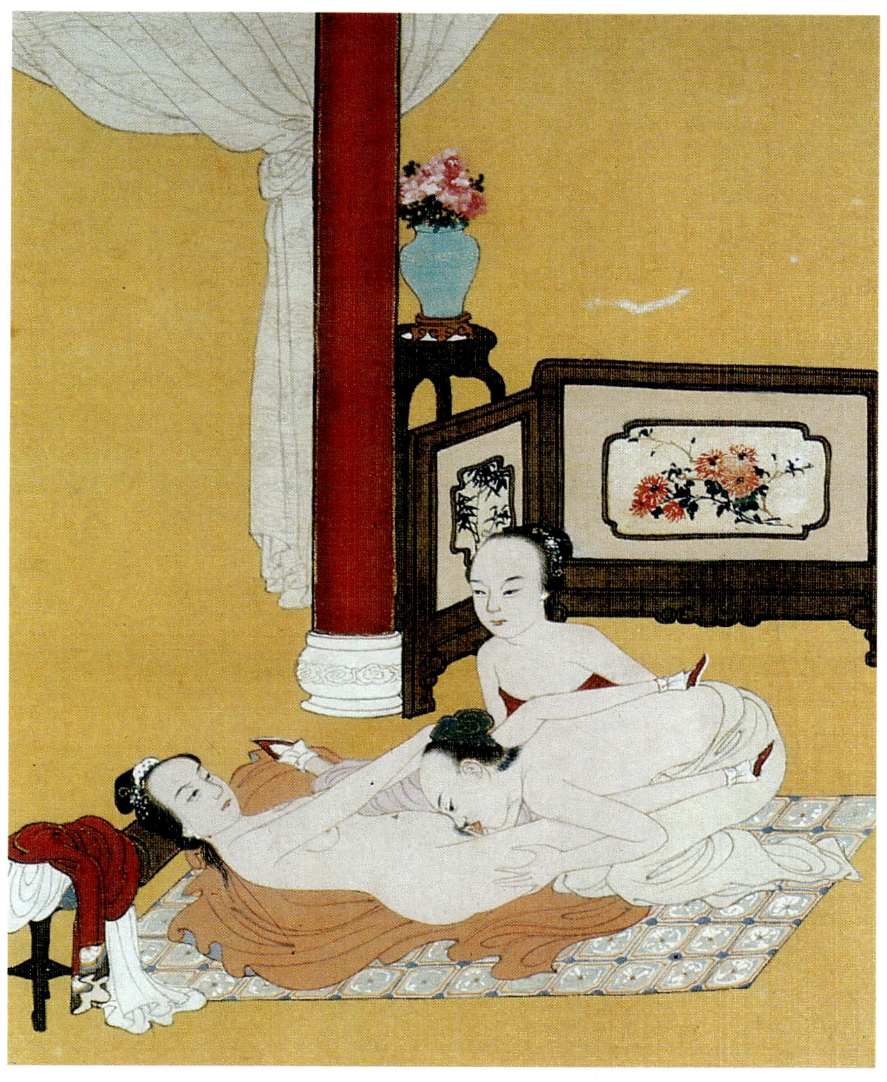

The dalliance scene has moved to a mat on the floor. A partly clothed Chinese man kneels before a reclining woman and probes her "Golden Crevice" with his tongue while a second woman sits in attendance. The subtle relationship of colors in this painting conveys a mood of intimate sensuality. Flowers blooming in a vase and on a screen near a crimson column symbolize the sexual satisfaction of the woman and the virility of the man.

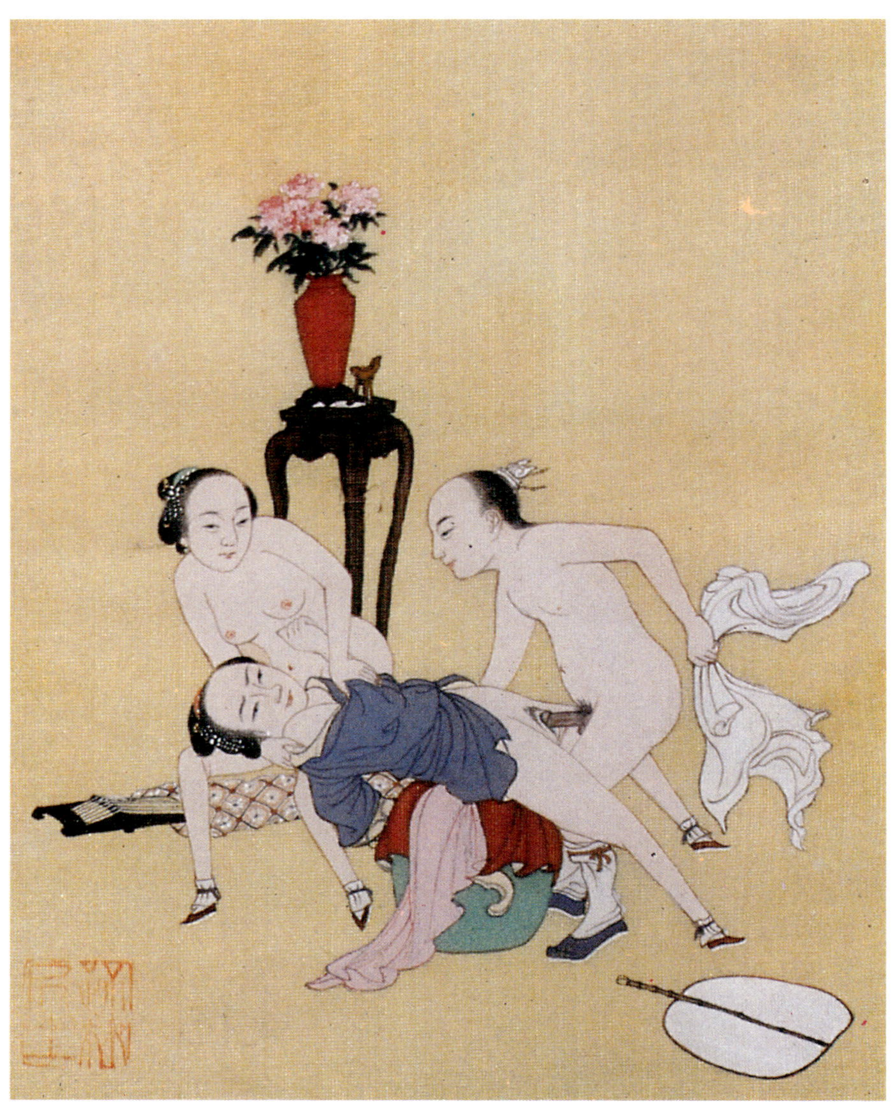

In this delicate Chinese painting a man unites with one woman who is partly supported by a second woman. This is a variation of the Taoist posture known as Queen Bee Making Honey. The pink flowers blooming in a vase over the heads of the participants suggest sexual satisfaction.

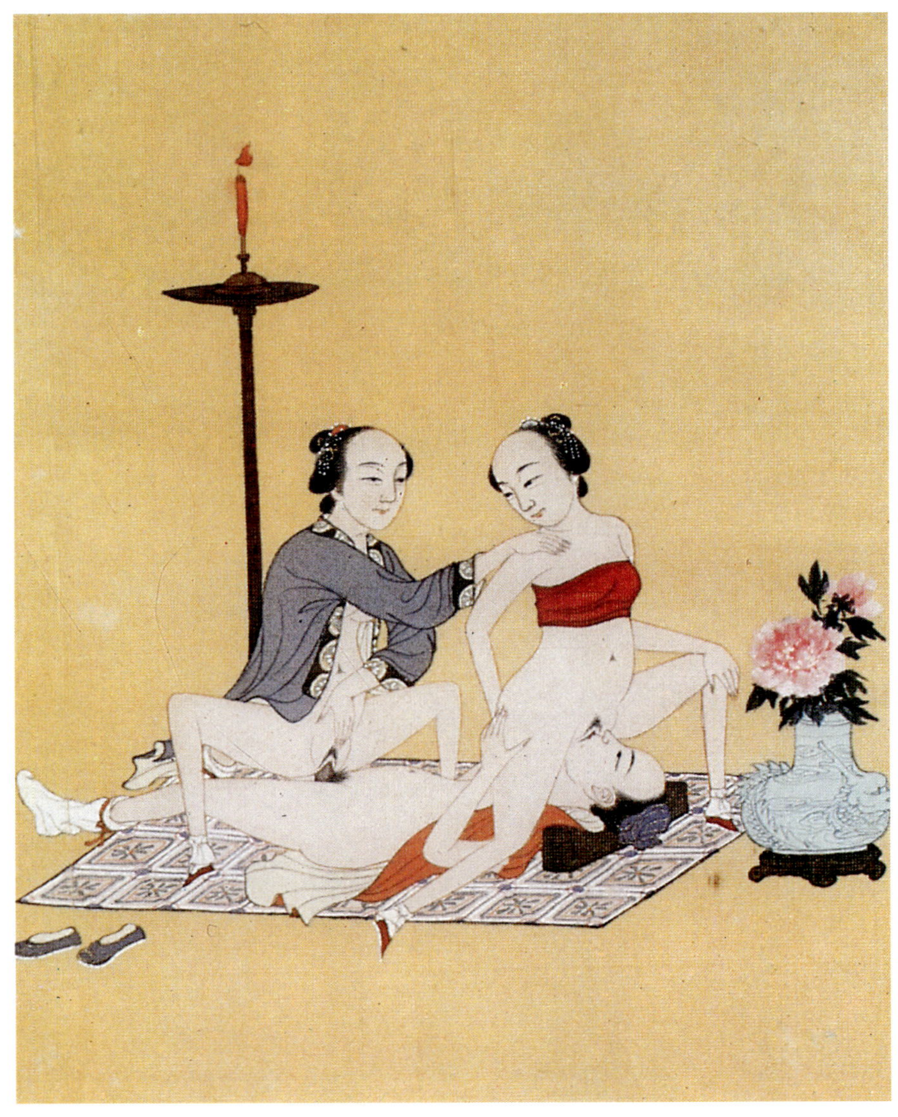

This depiction of Taoist love dalliance of the type known as Feast of Peonies shows a Chinese man reclining on a mat while two women make love to him; as one lowers her "Precious Flower" over his "Jade Stalk," the other presents her "Pleasure Grotto" to his mouth. The two blooming peonies in a jade dragon-motif vase emphasize the symbolic aspect of this sexual practice, designed to enhance the vitality of all participants.

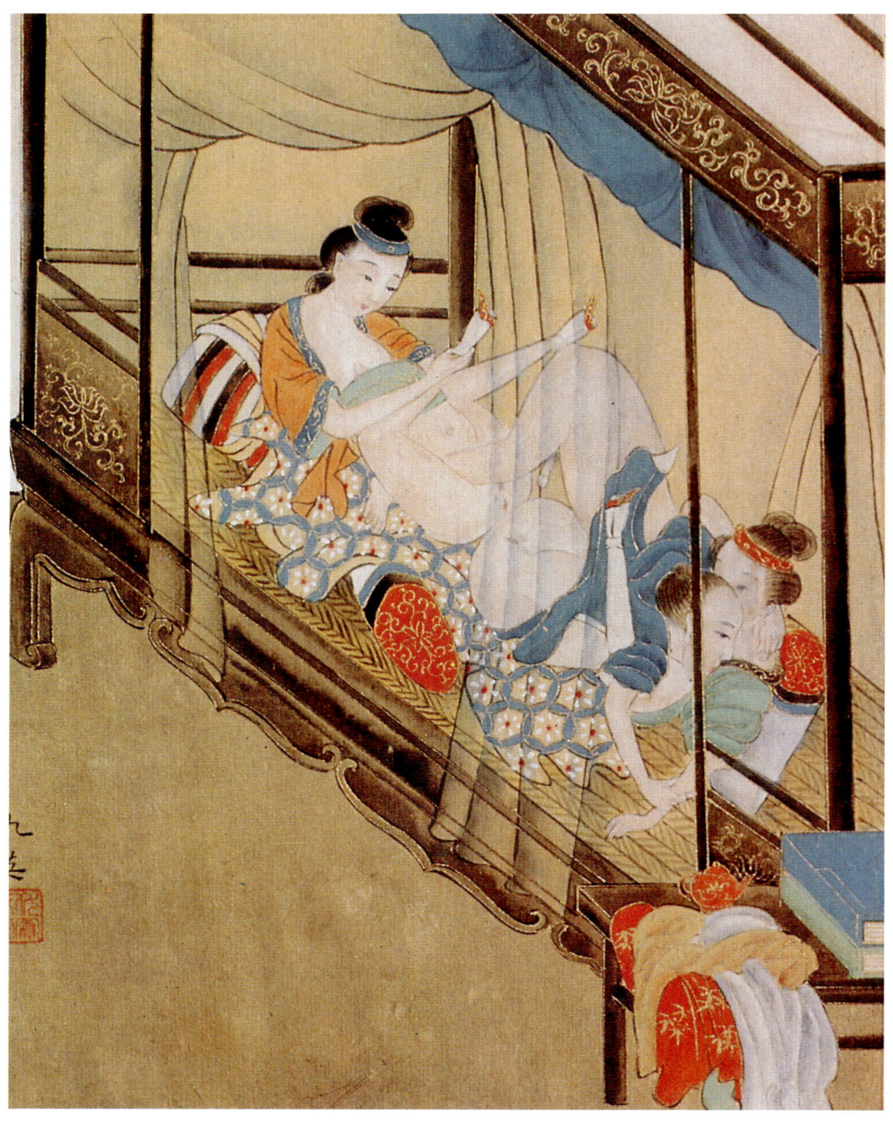

A Chinese man makes love with two women in an exotic canopied bed. They seem to be practicing a variation of the Taoist posture known as *Two Dancing Female Phoenix Birds;* discarded clothes and a pair of pillow books rest on a table in the foreground. A feeling of spontaneity is expressed by the clever use of color and composition.

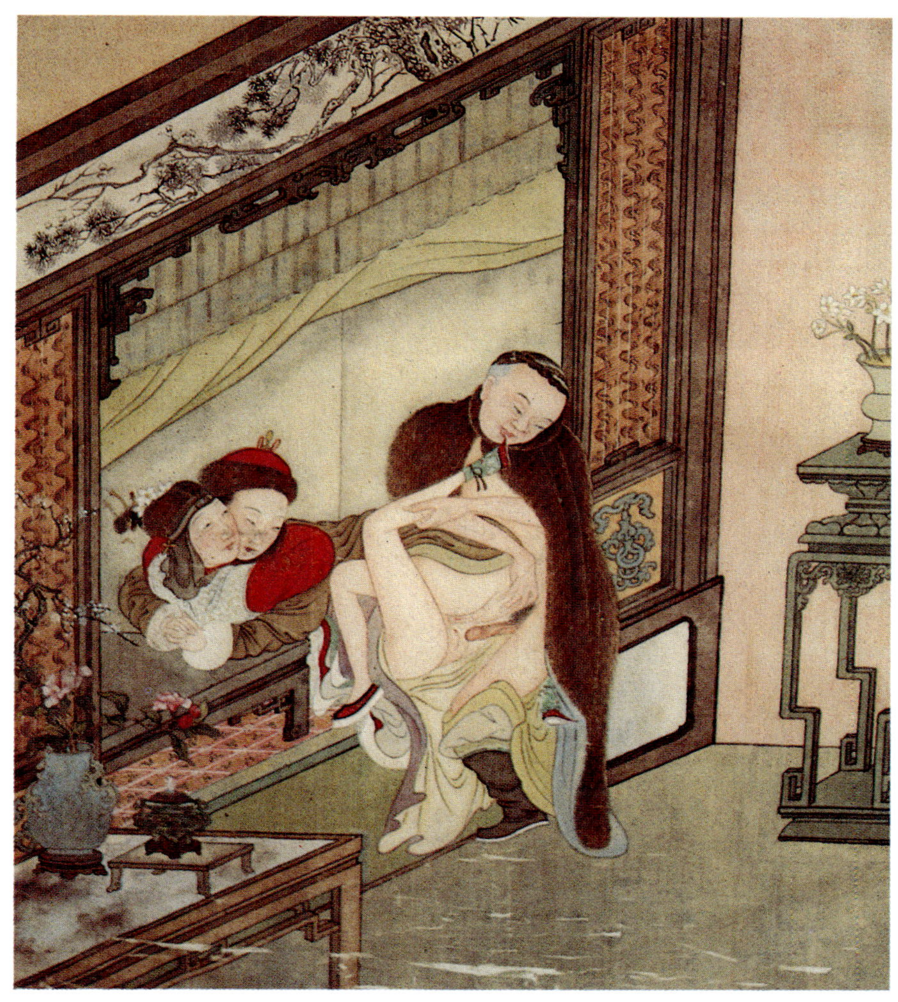

A Chinese fur-clad nobleman stands by an ornate canopied bed and is engaged in secret dalliance with two similarly clad ladies in close embrace. His "Jade Scepter" penetrates each "Jade Gate" in turn, in a version of the Taoist love posture known as *Two Dancing Female Phoenix Birds*. Vases filled with blooming flowers on nearby tables evoke the abundance of Yin and the potentizing power of Yang.

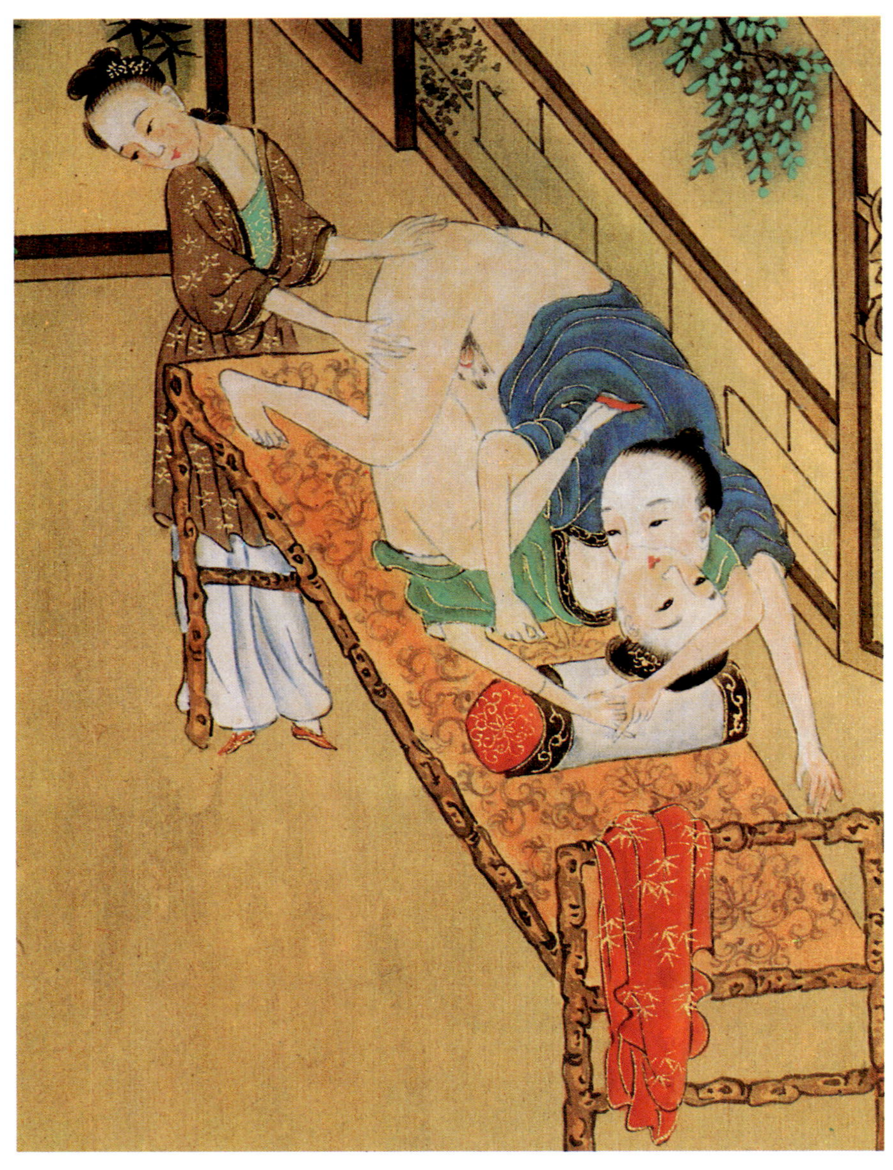

A Chinese couple are shown making love on a bamboo bed while a maidservant stands behind them and assists their love movements. This form of erotic dalliance is a version of the classical Taoist posture known as Jungle Fowl.

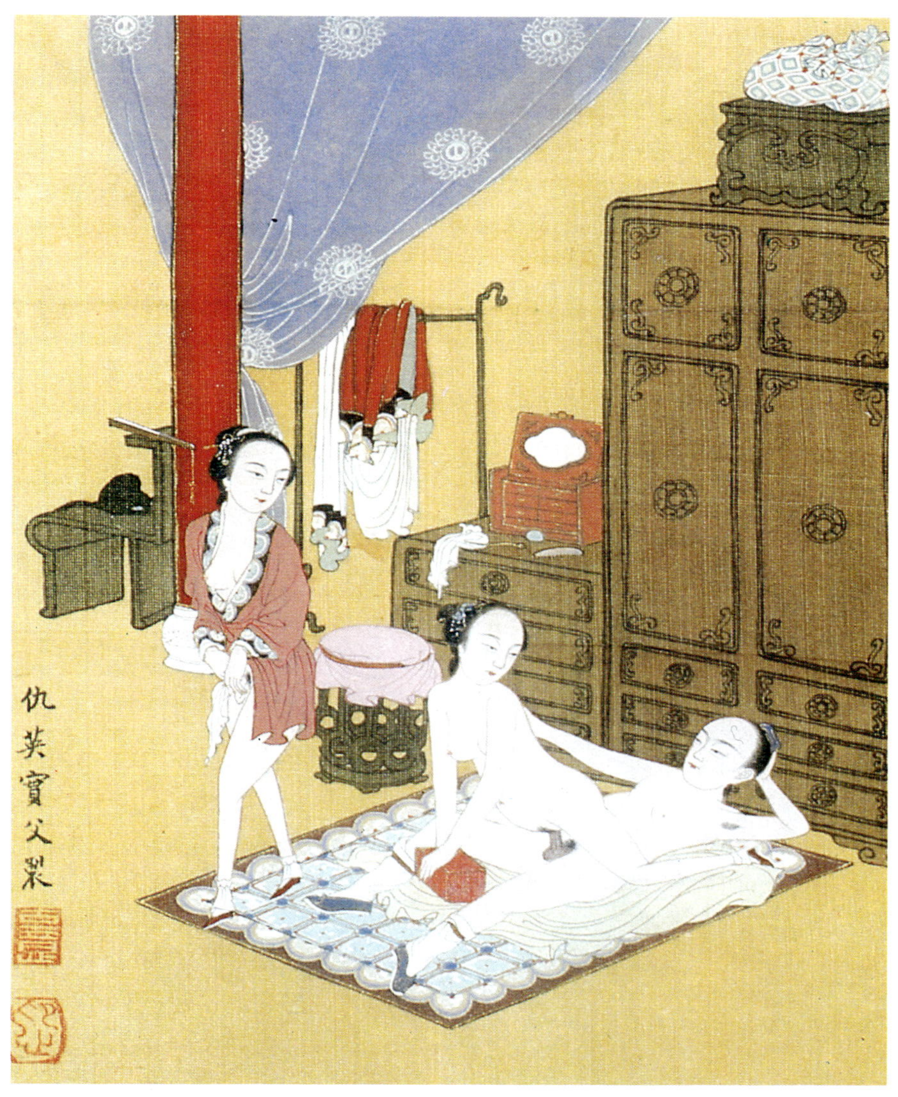

A Chinese man reclines on a sleeping mat as a woman straddles his body and performs the classic posture known as Reversed Flying Ducks. A second partly clothed woman is shown walking away from the scene, holding a love-cloth in her hands. Ornate cabinets are portrayed in the background.

BIBLIOGRAPHY

Beurdeley, Michel, et al. *The Clouds and the Rain: The Art of Love in China.* London: Hammond and Hammond, 1969.

Beurdeley, Michel, and Richard Lane, et al. *Erotic Art of Japan: The Pillow Poem.* Hong Kong: Leon Amiel, 1985.

Bowie, Theodore, and Cornelia V. Christenson. *Studies in Erotic Art.* New York: Basic Books, 1970.

Chang, Jolan. *The Tao of Love and Sex.* London: Wildwood House, 1977.

Chang, Stephen. *The Tao of Sexology.* San Francisco: Tao Publishing, 1986.

Chia, Mantak, and Maneewan Chia. *Healing Love through the Tao: Cultivating Female Sexual Energy.* New York: Healing Tao Books, 1986.

Chia, Mantak, and Michael Winn. *Taoist Secrets of Love: Cultivating Male Sexual Energy.* New York: Aurora Press, 1984.

Cleary, Thomas. *Immortal Sisters: Secrets of Taoist Women.* Boston: Shambhala, 1989.

Douglas, Nik. *The Art of Love.* Beverly Hills: Kreitman Gallery, 1979.

Douglas, Nik, and Penny Slinger. *Sexual Secrets: The Alchemy of Ecstasy (Special Edition).* Rochester, Vermont: Destiny Books, 1989.

Douglas, Nik, and Penny Slinger. *The Pillow Book: The Erotic Sentiment and the Paintings of India, Nepal, China and Japan.* New York: Destiny Books, 1981.

Douglas, Nik, and Penny Slinger. *The Erotic Sentiment in the Paintings of India and Nepal.* Rochester, Vermont: Park Street Press, 1989.

Egerton, Clement. *The Golden Lotus (The Chin P'ing Mei)* 4 volumes. London: Routledge and Kegan Paul, 1972.

Etiemble. *Yun Yu: An Essay on Eroticism and Love in China.* Geneva: Nagel, 1970.

Evans, Tom, and Mary Evans. *Shunga: The Art of Love in Japan.* New York: Paddington Press, 1975.

Franzblau, Abraham N. *Erotic Art of China.* New York: Crown, 1977.

Gerhard, Poul. *Pornography or Art?* Bishop's Stortford, England: Words and Pictures, 1971.

Gerhard, Poul. *The Pillow Book or a History of Naughty Pictures.* Bishop's Stortford, England: Words and Pictures, 1971.

Girchner, Lawrence E. *Erotic Aspects of Chinese Culture.* USA, private limited edition, 1957.

Gregersen, Edgar. *Sexual Practices: The Story of Human Sexuality.* London: Mitchell Beazley, 1982.

Grosbois, Charles. *Shunga: Images of Spring.* Geneva: Nagel, 1965.

Grove Press Editors. *Fille de Joie.* New York: Grove Press, 1967.

Humana, Charles, and Wang Wu. *The Chinese Way of Love.* Hong Kong: CFW Publications, 1982.

Ihara, Saikaku. *The Life of an Amorous Man: A Story of Erotic Adventure.* Rutland, Vermont: Charles E. Tuttle Company, 1964.

Illing, Richard. *Japanese Erotic Art: And the Life of the Courtesan.* New York: St. Martin's Press, 1979.

Ishihara, Akira, and Howard Levy. *The Tao of Sex: A Chinese Introduction to the Bedroom Arts.* New York: Harper and Row, 1970.

Kronhausen, Phyllis, and Eberhard Kronhausen. *The Complete Book of Erotic Art.* New York: Bell, 1978.

Kronhausen, Phyllis, and Eberhard Kronhausen. *Catalogue of the International Museum of Erotic Art.* San Francisco: National Sex Forum, 1973.

Kuhn, Franz. *The Before Midnight Scholar (Jou Pu Tuan of Li Yu).* London: Deutsch, 1965.

Levy, Howard. *Chinese Footbinding: The History of a Curious Erotic Custom.* London: Neville Spearman, 1966.

Levy, Howard. *The Illusory Flame.* Tokyo: Kenkyusha, 1962.

Levy, Howard. *Warm Soft Village.* Tokyo: Dai Nippon Insatsu, 1964.

Levy, Howard. *A Feast of Mist and Flowers: The Gay Quarters of Nanking at the End of the Ming.* Yokohama: private edition, 1966.

Maspero, H. *Le Taoism.* Paris: Publications Guimet, 1950.

Maspero, H. *Les Procedes de Nourir le Principe Vital dans la Religion Taoiste Ancienne.* Paris: Journal Asiatique, 1937.

Needham, Joseph. *History of Scientific Thought in Science and Civilization in Ancient China, Vol II.* Cambridge: Cambridge University Press, 1956.

Neuer, Roni, and Stephanie Kiceluk. *Shunga: The Erotic Art of Japan.* (1600–1979). New York: Ronin Gallery, 1979.

Pampaneu, J. *Erotologie de la Chine.* Paris: PK, 1963.

Piggott, Juliet. *Japanese Mythology.* London: Paul Hamlyn, 1969.

Rambach, Pierre. *The Art of Japanese Tantrism.* London: Macmillan, 1979.

Rawson, Philip. *Erotic Art of the East.* New York: Prometheus, 1968.

Reid, Daniel. *The Tao of Health, Sex and Longevity.* New York: Simon and Schuster, 1989.

Smith, Bradley. *Erotic Art of the Masters.* La Jolla, California: Gemini-Smith/Erotic Art Book Society, no date (?1974).

Soulie, Bernard. *Japanese Erotism.* New York: Crescent Books, 1981.

Van Gulik, Robert H. *Erotic Color Prints of the Ming Period.* Tokyo: privately printed limited edition, 1951.

Van Gulik, Robert H. *Sexual Life in Ancient China.* Leiden: Brill, 1974.

Yang, Richard, and Howard Levy. *Monks and Nuns in a Sea of Sins.* Washington: Sino-Japanese Sexology Classics, 1971.